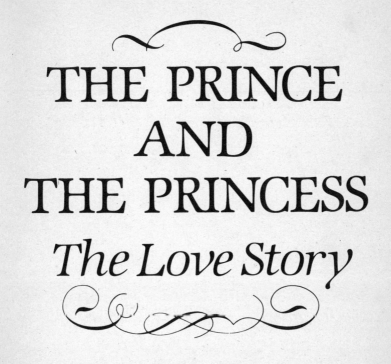

THE PRINCE
AND
THE PRINCESS
The Love Story

Norman King

A WALLABY BOOK
Published by Simon & Schuster
NEW YORK

Cariño—
Je t'aime, ma cherie

Author's note: Consistent with the growing tradition of "docu-drama," some of the dialogue contained in this book represents the dramatic recreation of events whose specific details are known only to the actual participants.

Published by Wallaby Books
A Simon & Schuster Division of Gulf & Western Corporation
Simon & Schuster Building
1230 Avenue of the Americas
New York, New York 10020
WALLABY and colophon are registered trademarks of Simon & Schuster
First Wallaby Books printing March 1983
3 5 7 9 10 8 6 4 2
Manufactured in the United States of America

Library of Congress Cataloging in Publication Data

King, Norman, date.
The Prince and the Princess.

"A Wallaby book."
1. Charles, Prince of Wales, 1948–   —Fiction.
2. Diana, Princess of Wales, 1961–   —Fiction.
I. Title.
PS3561.I4819P7   1983   813'.54   82-24869
ISBN 0-671-45784-5

THE PRINCE
AND
THE PRINCESS
The Love Story

1

Pheasant shooting at Althorp always became a noisy, brawling, festive occasion. Dogs yelped, shotguns banged, participants and spectators jested and cheered. Tweedy hunting rigs and shooting caps gave the assemblage on the estate of the eighth Earl Spencer the nostalgic quality of a nineteenth-century print.

On one biting, chilly, and overcast day in November, 1977, Lady Diana Spencer stood in jeans, gumboots, and sweater in the middle of a field recently plowed after harvest, swept up in the excitement and elegance of the ancient English tradition of pheasant shooting. It was the tradition that intrigued her; not the reality. For the sixteen years of her life she had never really reconciled herself to the bloodshed and sadism of the shoot. She had been born to it, suffered through it when necessary; she hated it.

Yet this time the pheasant shoot promised an exquisite bonus for Diana. She would be able to meet Prince Charles.

The Prince of Wales dated many girls—he had been seeing dozens of them over the past decade. Every day the newspapers carried lurid tales of his latest heart interest. His latest was Diana's older sister, Lady Sarah Spencer.

Sarah deliberately played it cool with Diana whenever Charles was the subject of discussion. It was a role Diana did not appreciate. She wondered what was *really* going on between Charles and her sister. Sarah had already told Diana—and her sister Jane as well—that Charles fell in love easily and out of love just as easily.

Diana had never let on how much she liked Charles. It was a private thing. Their age difference was an absolutely maddening twelve years and seven-and-a-half months— almost a generation gap. She didn't want to admit her crush on him—people would laugh. For years she had borne it in silence, every time she played with his younger brothers, Princes Andrew and Edward, with whom she was usually teamed up, even in the swimming pool at Park House in Sandringham when Charles was away at school and she was a mere infant.

The two of them—Prince Charles in his hunting jacket and cap, carrying his twin-barrel 12-bore shotgun, and Lady Sarah in a slightly overstyled pant suit—appeared suddenly at the border of the field. Several of the shooters had already formed up in the traditional shooting line across the rectangular field, but there was space in the middle left for Prince Charles and several other distinguished guests Diana's father had invited to the shoot that day.

Immediately Sarah saw Diana, a flash of annoyance shadowed her eyes. But she threw back her head to chat with Charles as they walked along toward Diana, hand in hand. Slim and elegant in his hunting gear, the Prince of Wales lowered his head to speak to Sarah. Imperceptibly, Sarah drew him away from Diana. Diana strode across the field resolutely to intercept them just about at the shooting line, her long legs swinging her body along spendidly.

Sarah was looking up at Charles adoringly; Charles was laughing. Dutifully? Diana hoped. How elegantly he held himself in those beautifully tailored clothes! He always looked better in uniform than in business rig; it was his build, apparently. At that moment, Sarah turned toward her sister, the annoyance in her face apparent and said:

"Oh, it's Diana." Pause. "You *know* my sister, of course."

Lady Diana drew herself up in front of Prince Charles, pulling her arms around her against the chill November wind which was cutting through the field. She felt awkward and all knobby knees now that she was close to him. She always felt clumsy and heavy around Sarah. Sarah was sylphlike and angelic compared to Diana. Diana was taller, more solid, more big-boned.

Charles's gaze fastened on her, his blue eyes probing directly into hers, his mouth twisted in a kind of raffish and expectant grin, tufts of brown curly hair escaping the cap and moving just a bit in the wind that was riffling the tops of the hedgerows.

"I should think it's Diana, isn't it?"

He was studying her with open interest, all over, from head to toe. She could feel those famous piercing blue eyes holding her in thrall. He seemed interested, she thought—*interested*. She was conscious of the fact that she was almost as tall as he. Automatically she shrank down just a bit, pulling herself earthward, her knees slightly turning in. He seemed bigger than life; he had always been older, more experienced, more powerful.

"You're not shooting?" he asked. "Abandoning your namesake?"

For a moment she panicked. What in the world was he talking about? Then it came to her—like a heaven-sent inspiration. She was not really very bright when it came to the classics. Diana was the classic Greek huntress. At least she did know that.

"I'm the *new* Diana," she laughed, trying to avoid her usual inane giggle. She had acquired the abominable habit of bursting out into giggles to hide any embarrassment or disappointment. It was not at all dignified. Both her father, Earl Spencer, and her mother, now married to another man, were trying to break her of it.

Charles smiled. She could feel the force of his masculinity, the tremendous power of his personality. An introverted person, he had spent the years of his growing up hardening himself physically and psychologically against adversity. In doing so, he erected a hard shell of reserve around himself. When he focused his attention on anyone, he achieved an intensity almost hypnotic to the uninitiated.

"You most certainly are the new Diana."

"Diana's home from *school* for the weekend," Sarah said slyly.

Giving her sister a withering look, Diana turned once again to Charles. "It's my last semester at West Heath," she said. "It's all so terribly dull. Absolutely maddening."

"Studying was never my strongest point," Charles observed thoughtfully.

Sarah took Diana by the arm. "Come on. We'd best leave the men to the shooting. I know how you *hate* blood sports."

Diana lifted her sister's fingers from her arm carefully. "I think I'll stay and watch, if you don't mind. *You* go on alone." It was almost a command.

Sarah's face was a complex of emotions. "You're staying?" She turned to Charles blandly. "Surely you don't want her here with you."

"It doesn't bother me," Charles said vaguely, examining his gun. He eyed Diana. "If you don't mind the noise."

"Not in the least."

Sarah turned on her heel and strode off across the field.

"Care to try a few shots?" the Prince of Wales asked Diana after a moment of silence.

"Never in a million years."

"You dislike shooting?"

"Sarah is right. I *hate* it."

Charles was amused. "Then why put yourself out?"

"It's something to do. I worked in the shop all yesterday. It's somebody else's turn."

Diana had been invited home for the weekend not only because the Prince of Wales was coming, but because she was required to work in her stepmother's souvenir shop at the rear of the Spencer stables, selling knick-knacks to tourists. When Diana came home, she usually chose to live in one of the guest cottages on the estate rather than in the main house. Along with her sisters, she was not on the friendliest of terms with Raine Spencer, their father's second wife.

Diana turned to see her father, stocky, ponderous, and slow-moving, coming across the field toward them, smiling amiably. He greeted the Prince of Wales, who returned the greeting affably. Then Earl Spencer frowned at his daughter.

"What are you doing out here, Duchess?"

She found herself blushing. She thought she had outgrown that family nickname long ago. "I thought I'd watch the shoot."

Her father didn't know quite what to make of that, perfectly aware that Diana loathed blood sports, but he shrugged his shoulders and went on his way.

"I think 'Duchess' is a nice name," Charles said, his eyes laughing.

"It's dreadful!" she said softly. "I don't know how I ever got it."

She did know, of course, It was given to her because she had a rather high and mighty way about her, at least she had when she wanted something badly. Usually easygoing and cheerful, she became cranky when crossed or deprived of what she desired.

Charles was not put off by her innocent disclaimer. He was about to question her when Earl Spencer's master of the shoot shouted down the line for them to prepare for the first flush of game.

Diana and Charles turned toward the hedgerow at the upper end of the plowed field. It was at the row of trees that the pheasants would appear. Diana knew exactly how they were driven out of their hiding places in the field beyond. There the beaters ran at the coverts to drive out the birds. The pheasants then flew up, away from the beaters, soaring over the tops of the trees and downhill toward the line of shooters. Pheasants flew high, straight, and fast; the best shots were taken by the shooters while the pheasants were directly overhead.

Almost immediately three birds rose. Diana held her breath. They flew so swiftly, so gracefully, so undeviatingly.

None of them came directly at Charles. He stood there, gun pointed down at the ground in front of him. There were several blasts. Diana wanted to hold her ears and cry, but she steeled herself against flinching. One of the pheasants plummeted to the ground ahead of the line. A second fell. The third survived to fly on behind them into a thicket.

Almost immediately another bird appeared at the row of trees, this one coming directly at Charles.

"Yours!" someone shouted.

Diana watched breathlessly as Charles quickly let the shotgun rise almost of its own accord, easily, effortlessly. With both eyes open, he sighted casually along the barrel of the shotgun and one barrel exploded. The pheasant was untouched. Instantly the second barrel went off. The bird fell.

"Good shot!"

"That was a rocketer," a voice said.

In shooting terms, a rocketer was a bird that flew high and fast toward its shooter.

After several more birds appeared, the retrievers were loosed to bring the carcasses back to the shooting line. Diana tried not to look at the dead bird that Charles had killed.

"Sarah says you don't ride," Charles observed during the lull in shooting.

"I had a bad fall when I was eight. I *can* ride."

"But you swim well, don't you?"

"Yes. I dance, too. And I *love* to ski."

"So does Sarah."

Diana knew that Sarah wanted to be invited to Klosters by Charles during the coming ski season. She tried not to think about that.

"If this is your last semester at school, what are you planning to do afterward?"

"I don't particularly know," Diana said. "I'm not a very good student. Although I like history."

"I liked history, too," Charles said.

"My father once told me it was because I kept reading about my relatives!"

Charles laughed.

"There was another Diana Spencer," she said with sudden enthusiasm. "She wanted to marry a Prince of Wales back in the time of George II."

Charles frowned. "That would be Frederick, the Prince of Wales. What happened?"

"The Prime Minister found out what was going on, and put a stop to it!"

"Oh," said Charles, "bad luck."

He turned quickly to take another rocketer that was sweeping over him. Conversation flagged. Then it picked up. They discussed other personal likes and dislikes, and found to their astonishment that neither one of them liked to drink much, except Charles could go an occasional glass of wine. But he didn't like tea, coffee, or red wine; Diana liked tea and coffee. Neither liked to smoke; neither tolerated it in others.

The day passed quickly. By the time it was almost over, Diana had drifted into a euphoric cloud. She left the shooting line before Charles was through and walked across the clods in the field, thinking about how wonderful he was, a pretty amazing man, just the way she had assumed he would be. She hoped he would remember her. Perhaps he might come back sometime to Althorp to see *her*, not Sarah. Perhaps he might look her up that evening, or the next day, before he left. Perhaps he would track her down in the garden at Althorp and tell her what an attractive person she was, how full of life, how vital, how jolly, how amusing.

Dreaming on, Lady Diana Spencer returned to her rooms in the guest house at Althorp and cleaned up. Later on, she wandered through the mansion that was now open to the weekend guests, looking with wonder at the hundreds of priceless paintings from the Spencer collection, reading the titles on the leather spines of the endless rows of books, studying the elegant furniture from other ages. the interior of the house was a fairybook illustration come true, a place where Diana could think about a happy ending to a romance that as yet was all in her head.

That evening, Diana watched as the Prince of Wales and Lady Sarah Spencer made a triumphal entry together, she on his arm, before the assembled guests in Althorp's magnificent dining room. Diana bit back her remorse and smiled gaily and happily as everyone saluted the attractive couple.

Nor did Charles seek out Diana before the weekend was over. She was not let down; she did not allow herself any self-pity. She simply made up her mind that she would manage another meeting with him. She did not have any idea how, but she was determined to do so.

Actually, the next meeting occurred without any effort on her part. Within weeks, the entire Spencer family was invited to Sandringham by the Queen; Charles was there.

To Diana, Sandringham was home. She had been born right there on the estate, at Park House, where her mother and father lived. At the time her father was Viscount Althorp, not Earl Spencer; he had once served as equerry, or attendant, to Queen Elizabeth II. Diana's maternal grandmother, Ruth, Lady Fermoy, was even now Lady-in-Waiting to the Queen Mother.

It was through her mother's side of the family, Lord and Lady Fermoy, that the Spencers had acquired entrée into Park House, which was actually part of the royal estate at Sandringham.

Only when her grandfather, the seventh Earl Spencer, died in 1975, did the family move from Park House to Althorp. At the time, Diana was away at school and her mother had already divorced her father and remarried.

Diana always thought of Park House with nostalgia. It had the only heated swimming pool on the estate. Often members of the royal family came in to use the pool. She never saw Charles. But she grew up with Princes Andrew and Edward. Andrew was only one year older than she, a handsome young boy, with a big smile and an outgoing manner that was quite the opposite of his older brother's. Charles was known to them all as "Jug-Ears."

Diana was usually paired off with Andrew; he never seemed to mind, nor did she. It was difficult not to get on with Andrew. As he grew up, he became more and more attractive and dashing. Everyone loved him, especially the ladies. Diana never fought the idea that she was Andrew's good friend.

But at the same time, Diana sensed that, deep within Charles, there was something very vulnerable, very wonderful, and very difficult to touch. On the outside he appeared stiff and shy. As he grew up he overcame that and seemed to become almost as extroverted and easygoing as Andrew.

It was only a pose. She knew he wasn't. Because he wasn't smooth, she loved him all the more. She herself had no hangups. There was a natural cheerfulness in her that was difficult to put down. Early on she had acquired a sense of duty; she thought that it was important to do one's chores and carry one's burden in life.

When she was six, her mother, who had been Frances Ruth Burke Roche before her marriage to Edward "Johnny" Spencer, suddenly disappeared. Then she applied for a divorce. That was in 1969. Sarah and Jane, Diana's older sisters, were shattered by the rupture. Diana was too young to understand the implications fully. Yet she realized that something disturbing was going on; she began biting her nails—a habit she never really outgrew.

A sensational divorce trial followed. The two families— her mother's and her father's—split down the middle. Some on both sides supported Frances Spencer and some Johnny Spencer. Diana's maternal grandmother, Ruth, Lady Fermoy—a headstrong and determined woman— refused to speak to her daughter—likewise headstrong and determined—ever again. The "royalists" supported Lady Fermoy; the "others" supported Diana's mother Frances. It was all very nasty and picayune.

Frances Roche Spencer remarried soon afterward, becoming Mrs. Peter Shand Kydd. It was at this time that Diana's grandmother, Lady Fermoy, left her position at the palace to assume the upbringing of the children whom their mother, in the words of some, "abandoned." There was always a close tie from that moment on between Diana and her grandmother. For many months Lady Fermoy was Diana's mother, and a mother to her two older sisters and younger brother.

After a disturbing trial for custody of the children, the court awarded them to Earl Spencer, depriving their mother of their charge. They were allowed to visit her, but their home was with Earl Spencer. For some time, however, none of the children did much traveling to be with their mother.

When Diana was six, she was a day pupil at Silfield School in King's Lynn for two years. Then, at the age of eight, she was sent to Riddlesworth Hall, a preparatory school near Diss in Norfolk, not far from Sandringham. She settled down, was good at games, and loved to swim. She even won a prize for effort from the headmistress when she left.

When she turned twelve, Diana changed to West Heath, a boarding school south of London near Sevenoaks in Kent, about a hundred miles from home. There she spent her teens quietly, by no means blossoming as a scholar.

Now, finally, at sixteen, she was once again at a crossroads in her life.

On the visit to Sandringham shortly after the memorable pheasant shoot at Althorp, Diana found Prince Charles with her sister Sarah most of the time. She did manage to catch his eyes once or twice, but nothing came of it for the first few nights. The tremendous press of guests sometimes made it difficult to get about easily.

But then suddenly one evening Prince Charles was standing at her side.

"You're still at West Heath?" Charles began, more or less to pick up the conversation he had dropped at Althorp.

"Actually I'm almost through with West Heath. I'm

thinking of Rougemont, although none of the family knows it yet."

Charles frowned.

"A Swiss finishing school. The Institut Alpin Videmanette." She explained that it was in the Upper Sarine Valley, close to Gstaad and Chateau d'Oex, the famous ski resorts. "Jet-set country. It's a great challenge."

Charles evinced interest—didn't he always? For a moment Diana was afraid he was patronizing her. But she really didn't care, even if he was indulging in fun. At least he was talking to her.

"I'd like to polish up my French," she told him.

"So you can meet a rich Frenchman?" Charles suggested.

"I'd like to do a little skiing." Diana looked at Charles directly. She knew he might invite Lady Sarah to Klosters in the Alps for a week of skiing. She wondered if he would comment on that.

"It's a great sport," he said enthusiastically.

" And maybe learn a few new dance steps," Diana went on. "I was a ballet student, you know, before I grew too tall."

"Too tall for what?" Charles wondered. "A squat ballet student?"

"Ballet dancers must be compact," Diana explained. "When my legs got too long, I switched. To the real thing. That's why I want to get into new steps."

Charles shrugged. "I didn't know there were any new dance steps—only variations on old ones."

"You're talking about ballroom dancing." She drew back. "Come, now! I'm talking about *dancing*. The very real thing!"

She was aware that she was teasing him, but she had gone too far to retreat. In an untenable position, the only way to go was full speed ahead.

She pulled him out of the lighted and crowded room onto

the concrete terrace. "Watch me."

He did. She put together a few basic tap-dance steps she had learned—that's what she had meant in her teasing way to be "the real thing"—and ended up with a triumphant and flamboyant music-hall finish. He was watching her with disbelief.

"If you think it's easy, why don't you do it yourself?" she dared him.

"Why not?"

When he tried, it was a total disaster.

"Like this." She showed him the basic moves again. He tried them several times and after a moment had almost mastered the step. By now Diana was giggling without restraint. She did not notice that there were others now watching the two of them from inside. Several drifted out for a closer look.

"Now together," Diana said, taking his hand, and leading him back and forth over the terrace in a kind of low Irish clog. By now there was general laughter all around. When Charles finally finished, he had lost his balance and almost fallen. The two of them dissolved into mirth and the crowd applauded.

When it was over and Diana looked back on the scene, she was filled with embarrassment. Obviously she had handled the situation badly. She *should* have been a bit more ladylike. In fact, it was with the intention of apologizing that Diana looked up her sister Sarah after returning home to Althorp.

"Why ever apologize?" Sarah asked coolly.

Diana was surprised at her sister's tone of voice; she was obviously annoyed at Diana's interlude with Charles.

"He thought you were simply adorable," Sarah went on, an edge to her voice. "One of my friends described you as a cuddly little puppy, full of vitality and terribly sweet."

Diana flushed. She had not realized how Sarah felt about

her episode with Charles. "Oh, that's quite dreadful! I'm sorry, Sarah."

"There's nothing to be sorry about," Sarah said breezily. "You did make an impression, which I'm sure is what you *wanted* to do."

"But not *that* way."

"Charles is a good sport," Sarah told Diana succinctly. "He has a kind of zany sense of humor. It quite escapes me, but I *do* understand it." She eyed Diana. "It reminds me of yours, actually."

"Sarah, please," Diana began.

"I'm leaving within the week for Klosters with Charles," Sarah said airily. "We're going skiing."

In spite of the effect of the barb Sarah had just sunk, Diana tried to carry off the news with a bright smile. Yet why should she be at all surprised? Charles still thought of her as a child, just as her parents and Sarah did.

It did not make Diana sleep any better. Besides, there was always the big question of her education coming up. At sixteen, that was a major problem for any young woman. And Diana did not really know what to do about it.

2

By late 1977, Althorp had begun to settle down after two stormy years of change, upheaval, and dissension. The travail had occurred in 1975, on the death of the seventh Earl Spencer, Diana's grandfather.

As the eighth Earl, her father had begun the complicated process of moving his household from Park House to Northamptonshire. With both Sarah and Jane in and out in their busy lives, and with Diana's younger brother Charles away at school like Diana, most of the work fell on the servants and friends. Diana came home as often as she could, trying to help her father get a grip on the management of the enormous estate.

Moving took place during most of 1975. Diana's father had help from an unexpected source. His old friend from Eton, Gerald Legge, had become the Earl of Dartmouth. Diana's father, always called "Johnny" by his friends, saw a lot of Gerald and Gerald's wife Raine. It was during those hectic months when Diana's father was getting used to being the eighth Earl Spencer that he grew closer and closer to Raine Legge.

Diana and her sisters and brother did not take to their father's new acquaintance. Diana herself felt Raine was far too energetic.a person to get along with easily. She preferred a more low-keyed individual. Raine came about her energy honestly. While she did not have a pedigree as pure as her husband's or Diana's, she did have a formidable parent.

Her mother was Barbara Cartland, a writer of romantic novels, probably the most prolific and successful of all modern romance writers. Raine's mother had married Alexander McCorquodale; then in mid-career, when she was in her thirties and just before World War II, Barbara McCorquodale divorced Raine's father and married his first cousin, Hugh McCorquodale!

None of this bothered Raine at all. Suffused with the same energy level as her famous mother, she became, after World War II, a do-gooder whose welfare work made her name a household word all over England. In her early twenties she had become the youngest member of the Greater London Council from the Borough of Westminster.

Diana could remember people talking about Raine even before her father had brought her home to introduce her to the children. She was a health fanatic and had been all her life. Stories about her appeared regularly in the tabloids. She took after her mother with that inborn ability to secure press space. From the first Diana was suspicious of her hold over Earl Spencer. But it was not up to Diana to discuss private affairs with her father.

Her sisters did. Diana could remember long arguments in the house about Raine even before she became a fixture there. Diana tried to shut out the dissension; in a way, she found life at school in Kent a lot easier than life at home. It was about that time, she remembered, that she began to see her real mother more often.

Her stepfather, Peter Shand Kydd, owned a number of cattle farms in Scotland and Australia. The Shand Kydds lived on a farm on the island of Seil, in the Firth of Lorne, sixty miles west of Glasgow. Diana found herself visiting her mother frequently; she loved the freedom and solitude of Seil. There were animals of all kinds on the farm. She quickly became attached to dogs and ponies. She also took up mackerel fishing and even learned to pot lobsters.

The move to Althorp had been completed and Diana's father was beginning to smooth things out when another earthquake struck. Quite suddenly, almost out of the blue, Raine Legge appeared at the manor one night and did not leave. Diana was away in school when this event happened.

"Raine's moved in!" Sarah told Diana on the phone.

"Moved in?"

"She's here."

"How long?"

"For good."

It was true. Raine was at Althorp for good. Her husband the Earl of Dartmouth knew this, and he decided that his old friend from Eton was the cause of the trouble. He instituted a divorce action in which he and Earl Spencer fought bitterly in court and in print.

One accused the other of adultery; the charges made all the gossip columns and Fleet Street's circulation soared for days. The judge eventually granted the Earl of Dartmouth a decree of divorce due to his wife's adultery "with a man against whom the charge has not been proved."

Diana had no idea what all that meant, but it seemed to imply that her father was at fault, but perhaps not legally.

The divorce was granted and things calmed down a bit. Diana and her sisters hoped that the air would clear and that Raine would go away.

She did not.

Within two months of the divorce, Diana's father married Raine. Diana was not at the wedding, nor were Sarah, Jane, or Charles. The nuptials were celebrated minimally, with only two witnesses.

Diana read about the wedding in the tabloids. No one in the family would talk about it. Diana was not at Althorp much during those weeks, but her sisters were. An undeclared feud was raging between the Spencer children and the new bride. Siding with the Spencer children were members of the house staff.

It got so bad that Diana would read about the feud in the newspapers. In one interview Raine complained to her mother, Barbara Cartland: "They won't accept me. Whatever I do is wrong. I just want us to be one close family."

Diana was appalled at all the publicity about matters that were personal and private. She spent most of her time at Sevenoaks minding her Ps and Qs, rising at seven-thirty every morning to the rising bell, eating her boiled egg for breakfast, and then studying throughout the day until seven in the evening.

But things were in a state of flux at Althorp. Diana heard from Sarah that Raine had begun to weed out members of the house staff who had been at the estate for years with their grandfather, the seventh Earl. In addition to that, Raine rolled up her sleeves and opened the house to the public as it had been open before, setting up guided tours through the magnificent rooms loaded with art treasures and cultural objets d'art from centuries before.

At the rear of the stables, she set up a souvenir shop where she sold trinkets and costume jewelry and china. She even opened up a tea shop to take care of visitors; it had a king-of-English-style, fast-food air to it.

Raine's ascension was not accepted wholeheartedly by the friends and neighbors of Earl Spencer. Anecdotes circulated by word of mouth and in the press. At one Northamptonshire dinner table, the host sat in silence next to the Countess Spencer, as Raine was now titled, during the entire first course of dinner. Raine continued to prattle on in her own breathless nonstop manner. Suddenly he turned to her and inquired:

"What did you say your name was? Storm?"

"No, Raine," said the Countess.

"Yes," the host said in a plummy British upperclass accent. "Knew it had something to do with the weather."

Still, when Diana was home on weekends or holidays, she did not really mind her stepmother. She worked for her in the curios shop out behind the stables, though she did usually stay at one of the guest houses. She managed to get along with her as well as could reasonably be expected, even if she was not on particularly intimate terms with her.

But now she was sixteen. She was finishing up at West Heath. Eleven years of schooling had proved that she was no great scholar. What should she do when she was no longer enrolled at West Heath in Kent?

Instead of asking her father and Raine for advice, Diana did what she had become used to doing when she wanted parental advice: she went to her mother and her stepfather. When they stayed in London, the Shand Kydds lived in an elegant apartment in Cadogan Place.

In the lovely sitting room that the Shand Kydds had furnished in a stylish kind of eclectic modern—a compatible mixture of traditional English furnishings and a few antiques—she sat facing both her mother and her stepfather. Elegant gilt-framed oil paintings of landscapes and portraits looked down at her from the walls. The decor was tasteful, expensive, and just exactly what it should be.

"You've developed into a very attractive young lady," her stepfather told her, smiling rather contentedly as if he had something to do with the transformation. "Now, whatever are we going to do with you?"

"It's pretty obvious I'm *not* the scholarly type."

"Thank heavens," her mother sighed. "I know too many ugly boffins to be impressed by brains."

Shand Kydd drummed his fingers on the surface of a beautiful Queen Anne table. "You could come out, you know."

Diana shook her head vigorously. "Much too dreadful. I don't want to go through that."

Frances raised an eyebrow. "Too much competition?"

"No. I simply think it's all too much fuss over nothing. It's really not in fashion anymore."

Shand Kydd considered. "I hardly think four years of University would suit you."

Diana paled. "I'd rather die!"

Frances fingered a long strand of beads. "What is it you'd like to do?"

Diana had thought about this long and hard. What she would like to do, of course, would be to marry Charles, but there was no use confessing that to her mother. And there was no sense pretending that she would immediately marry the first man who presented himself. She did not want just any man. She wanted the right man. She even knew who he was. At least, she would hold out for him until he was out of the running.

But she did not express any of these thoughts. "I had always thought I would be good with children," she said quietly. "Young children. I like them. I like to take care of them."

Frances frowned. "They won't let you begin teaching unless you have more training."

"I don't think University—"

Frances had a far-off look in her eye. "Duchess," she mused, "what about a good finishing school? You can sharpen up your French. You can learn the graces."

"She *knows* the graces," Shand Kydd snapped. "But I think that may be a way out." He turned to Diana. "What do you think?"

"I think—yes."

"You have one in mind?" Shand Kydd asked.

"Yes. The Institut Alpin Videmanette."

Frances approved. "They won't work you to death. The atmosphere's first-class."

"I'll only want a three-month course. Cooking, sewing, a little French."

"If you like it, you can always go on for the full course."

Diana nodded. "Yes, *if*."

Frances thought a moment. She turned to her husband. "What do you say?"

He agreed. The Shand Kydds put up a thousand pounds for the three-month term and once she had left West Heath, Diana was on her way.

Within days of her arrival that winter in Rougemont, Diana knew that she had been right to sign up for just the three-month course. It was not that there was anything wrong with the school—it was a model of Swiss finishing schools for the affluent and the titled—but she did not realize how much she missed England and home until she was away from them.

She loved to ski, so she polished up her abilities on the slopes with her companions. And she used her French not only in class but in the streets and shops of Rougemont as well. She took her classes in domestic science—

dressmaking and cooking. In a way, dressmaking and cooking were twin bores.

But she did manage to whip up the specialties of the house like cheese and meat fondues. And in a dressmaking class, she made a blouse or two of her own—frilly things which brought out the femininity which slacks and jackets lacked.

Still she suffered over her unrequited love for Prince Charles—in secret.

It didn't help to read about Prince Charles and Lady Sarah Spencer in the gossip columns. During their stay at Klosters in the nearby Alps, reams and reams of print told about their daily doings on the slopes, in the cafés, and at the chalet. There were also lengthy speculations about what went on in that tiny chalet at night, where both of them were staying. Diana felt the press was going a bit too far and that their minds were nasty, but she knew that her sister had actually let herself in for that kind of treatment by going with Charles to Klosters.

Most telling of all were photographs of Sarah and Charles coming out of the chalet in the morning, and going back in at night. The pictures of them driving about, sitting at bars, eating in cafés, holding their skis on the slopes, meant much less than those private photos in the doorway of the chalet.

Once their holiday was over, they were back in London, and Charles was squiring her about at the famous night spots and at West End theaters where hit shows were playing. Diana had been able to push all thoughts of Charles to the back of her mind, but now, with all the newspapers and magazines pushing him out at her, she realized that she was missing him terribly.

She also began to wonder about her sister and Charles. Her companions at the school constantly questioned her about Sarah and Charles.

"Is he going to marry her?"

"I have no idea."

"Ask her!"

She had never really made an issue of the romance she was imagining with Charles, but now it began to hurt. With all the pictures of the two of them in London doing the high spots, Diana became homesick. She was a grown-up woman now. Why was she wasting her time with French cooking and Swiss cuisine? Was she going to marry a Frenchman or a Swiss burgher?

On one of her loneliest days she found herself wandering along a sidewalk outside a kindergarten facility near the school. There were dozens of little girls running around in black-and-white uniforms.

Diana sat down to watch them. Two of the little girls came over to her immediately. She began practicing her French on them. They got along famously together. One child climbed up on her lap. The other recited a French poem to her.

Were they trying to break her heart? She left the playground, tears in her eyes. Easter was coming. Only six weeks of her three months were over. She flew back to England and never returned.

Frances saw Diana's action of leaving school as symptomatic of the times. Above all, she wanted her daughter to be happy, and if dropping out was the way to achieve her ends, it would have to be.

But she wanted to know more about why Diana had withdrawn. "Too much snobbery?" she asked.

"No," Diana said honestly. "It just isn't for me."

"And you don't want to come out," Frances went on. "You said that before."

No, Diana agreed. Neither Sarah nor Jane had come out; she wouldn't either, not for anything.

Shand Kydd was puzzled. "If you don't want to study and if you don't want to come out, what is there left?"

Frances eyed Diana with a half smile. "It's obvious to me."

Shand Kydd threw up his hands.

"She goes to work."

"At what kind of job?" Shand Kydd wondered.

Diana broke in. "I'll find something. All the women my age are working. It's the thing to do."

Frances nodded approval. "Peter and I are going to Australia soon for the autumn. I'll let you take the apartment here while we're gone."

Diana thanked her. "I'll look around for something while you're away. By the time you return, I'll be in my own place."

Shand Kydd asked, "Who's going to pay for that?"

"I'll ask Daddy."

"You won't want to live here alone, Diana." Frances' eyes lit up. "I know just the companion for you. Sophie Kimball is looking for rooms, too. Why don't the two of you live here until you both locate something?" Sophie Kimball was the daughter of Marcus Kimball, a Tory Member of Parliament.

It was agreed, and when the Shand Kydds flew down to their Australian farm in New South Wales, Diana and Sophie moved into the charming Cadogan Place apartment. They spent only three months together. Diana convinced her father that she should have a place in London, and he helped her find rooms in Old Brompton Road in the Earl's Court section of town, not far from Knightsbridge.

The apartment was in a long, extensive line of buildings called Coleherne Court; the rooms were at Number 60 in Section H, on the corner, overlooking the public library. The apartment dated back to 1901, constructed on the former site of Coleherne House and Hereford House. The available rooms, on the first floor, were going for one hundred thousand pounds—about $200,000—expensive, but well within Earl Spencer's budget. The rooms became Diana's home in London. Sophie had found another place, and she and Diana parted.

The new digs were far too large for Diana to manage herself. She got in touch first with Carolyn Pride, whom she had met at West Heath. When she told Carolyn what she was doing and where she was going to live, she immediately had herself a roommate. With Carolyn's help, she added two more people to share the costs: Anne Bolton and Virginia Pitman. Anne, the daughter of an Oxford brigadier general, was a secretary with Savills, a Mayfair estate agency. Virginia was in the same category as Diana; she did not have a job of any special kind but she was adept at mending china and did part-time work. Carolyn was pursuing her career in music.

It took time to settle in and get used to one another. Diana was the landlady, since the rooms were actually owned by her father. Carolyn was a no-nonsense type who became more or less Diana's executive officer. No one ever forgot it was Diana who was chairman of the board.

3

Life at 60 Coleherne Court was a challenge to Diana Spencer, but she quickly adjusted to the life of the working girl in London's more posh section. She and her friends were hardly the general run of London's stenos and typists from the middle class; the women she associated with were strictly the cream of the upper class.

It might be difficult to get the *right* job, but it was not difficult to get *any* job. Before going to work, Diana even took a fling at studying again—this time with a course in cookery at Cordon Bleu. It didn't last too long, but it did give her a few exotic strings for her cuisinery bow.

She got one job as an assistant to a catering group helping to cook for dinner parties. She made about $5.25 an hour. Cooking was not the most rewarding work she had ever done; she decided soon enough that it was not really her thing. She quit that job and went out looking for something else.

"What do you *really* want to do?" Carolyn Pride asked her. "I didn't think cooking would be a favorite pastime for you."

"I want to work with children," Diana admitted. "But I don't have a teaching degree."

"Why don't you get a job as a baby-sitter?"

"You mean for my relatives?" Diana asked, aghast.

"No, no. I mean through a professional agency. There *are* baby-sitting agencies, you know."

One of the first jobs she got through the agency was for an American couple named Robertson. Diana was hired to look after Patrick, the Robertsons' baby son, while the Robertsons were in London. The Robertsons liked her, she learned, because she was so "refined and well educated." Diana had no difficulty in getting along with little Patrick.

It was during her work with the Robertsons that Diana was invited to Buckingham Palace. The Robertsons were not happy that she would be unable to fulfill her day's work with young Patrick.

"I'm sorry," she told them when she returned after her day off.

No comment. Icy silence.

"I was being presented to the Queen."

Sensation. And many questions.

No one asked her about Prince Charles. She had not seen him, actually. Perhaps next time.

Diana worked for the Robertsons until they returned to New York when Patrick Robertson, Senior's job assignment in London ended.

Meanwhile, Diana was using her time in London to good advantage, experimenting with her dress. One of her main delights was in trying out new clothes. Being tall, she was an excellent model.

She discovered that she had a definite feel for clothes.

Her country-style taste, combined with a Londoner's sense of high style, shaped her clothes repertoire into something rich and strange. She loved corduroy culottes; they reminded her of the jeans and riding habits she wore at home. She loved lambswool sweaters, too, and bought dozens of them. Her favorite combination was to wear a cotton skirt and shirt from Laura Ashley. Her dresses and suits came from her favorite store, Harrods.

During this period of her life she began buying from a newly established firm of young designers in fashionable Mayfair named David and Elizabeth Emanuel. Her particular skin coloring and glowing health precluded the use of too much jewelry; she kept it simple and to a minimum.

Shortly after she had moved to London she received a telephone call from her sister Lady Jane.

"Robert and I are being married."

Diana wished her sister the best. Robert Fellowes was Assistant Private Secretary to the Queen, and had served as such since the year before. He was the son of Sir William Fellowes, for many years the Land Agent at Sandringham, where Diana was born. Naturally she knew Robert very well.

"I want you to be one of my bridesmaids."

"I'd love it!" Diana told her.

It was an exciting wedding, and directly after the honeymoon, the newlyweds moved into The Barracks at Kensington Palace, in the heart of London, where Robert could be close to Buckingham Palace. Many of the Palace staff members lived at Kensington Palace—a huge old house at the western end of Kensington Gardens, just north of Knightsbridge.

The most exciting thing to happen to Diana during her first days in London was that she passed her driver's test. She had little trouble; she was well coordinated and had a flair for getting about. As soon as she had her license and bought a blue Volkswagen she tooled it around the city like an expert.

"You handle that car like a racing driver," Carolyn told her one day after a harrowing ride back from visiting a friend.

"That doesn't sound like a compliment," Diana complained.

"It isn't, I assure you!" Carolyn told her sharply.

Diana spent holidays with her mother on the island of Seil when she could, but more and more her life was centered around London. She was maturing rapidly. Having settled in town with a particular circle of friends with whom she had good rapport and found compatible, she was becoming a poised young lady, corduroy culottes, lambswool sweaters, and all.

Her high spirits and her joy of living did not desert her now. She loved being in London—the beat of the city was in consonance with the beat of her own heart. It lent a certain excitement and ebullience to her lifestyle.

She began dating various men she met here and there. Besides running into people at parties on weekends in the country, she began getting telephone calls from men she had known through family ties. There were plenty of dates now, doing the night spots in London.

Most of the men in her life came from estate agencies, the wine trade or the auction houses. She favored restaurants like the Poule au Pot on Ebury Street and Topolino d'Ischia on Draycott Avenue. Her friends were discreet and their names did not usually appear in the gossip columns.

She met plenty of people her own age, but she tired quickly of doing the town in the manner of many of her peers. She preferred a quieter element than the discotheques and swinging parties that abounded in the London area. Noise and "the beat" were not actually her style. She was far from subdued, but she did tend to keep to herself. At times, in fact, when there was no one around, she would simply turn on the radio and dance around the apartment, bopping around, as she called it.

Among her dates were Harry Herbert, a stockbroker and the son of the Queen's racing manager Lord Porchester; Simon Berry, of the wine trade; and Humphrey Butler of Christie's. The man who dated her the most was James Boughey, a member of the Coldstream Guards who played cricket for Eton. But occasionally she went out with George Plumptre, a son of Lord FitzWalter.

To keep her independent there was always that nagging memory of Prince Charles to haunt her dreams and lurk in her thoughts. She knew he was still seeing Sarah—and other girls as well. Sarah did not discuss her dates with Charles as much now as she had at one time. Diana did not know why. She guessed that perhaps something had gone wrong between them, but she did not ask.

Prince Charles was notorious as a "swinger," in the term of the era. He dated women from almost every corner of the empire—and even on the continent. Ever since Diana could remember, Charles's conquests with women had been featured in the gossip columns of all the tabloids and magazines sold in London. His repertoire was enormous. It included royalty of many different countries, show business personalities, and even commoners of all sorts.

In fact, just before he had begun to take an interest in Lady Sarah Spencer, Charles had been involved in an international fiasco that caused ripples of excitement, disappointment, and even amusement in various places.

It all began when the Queen returned from a visit to Luxembourg in November, 1976. She came back with a most positive reaction to the Grand Duke Jean's daughter, Princess Marie-Astrid of Luxembourg. Shortly after that, she called her son in and discussed a meeting.

Prince Charles was still in the service at that time, commanding the H.M.S. *Bronington*. Doing what his mother had suggested he do, he docked the cruiser at Ostend, met his father, the Duke of Edinburgh, and drove up to Laeken Palace for a meeting with the Princess.

Diana had it from palace intimates that the meeting went very nicely. The Princess was twenty-three years old and quite pretty, in the same vein that movie actress Sonja Henie had been pretty many years before. Diana had seen her movies on television. Princess Marie-Astrid was adept at English, having mastered the language two years before.

Along with Marie-Astrid was her sister Margaretha. The group had a pleasant chat and luncheon at the Palace. Shortly after that, Charles and his father left for the dock, and the Commander of the *Bronington* shipped out on his regular schedule.

There was only one problem with such a liaison. Marie-Astrid was a Catholic. Being Catholic was indeed a problem for a potential wife of Prince Charles. There was, quite simply, a law against it. That law dated back to the Bill of Rights in 1789, which stated that the sovereign of England was not allowed to marry a Catholic; if Charles did so, he could not become king.

However, such a complication could be unraveled through negotiations. Rumors surfaced that such "negotiations" were being discussed in the highest circles of the British government. The eager press turned the rumors into facts, and on June 17 the *Daily Express* blew the lid off the case. It ran a headline:

CHARLES TO MARRY ASTRID—OFFICIAL

The story said: "Prince Charles is to marry Princess Marie-Astrid of Luxembourg. The formal engagement will be announced from Buckingham Palace on Monday. The couple's difference of religion will be overcome by a novel constitutional arrangement: any sons of the marriage will be brought up according to the Church of England, while daughters will be raised in the Catholic faith."

The news, the story said, was leaked from the royal family. Diana knew differently. There was no truth to the story at all. The actual source was never traced. In the United States, such a story might have been called a trial balloon.

But Prince Charles immediately issued a denial through the Queen's then press secretary Ronald Allison:

"I am authorized by His Royal Highness the Prince of Wales to make the following statement. There is no truth at all in the report that there is to be an announcement of an engagement of the Prince of Wales to Princess Marie-Astrid of Luxembourg."

The whole thing blew over.

Later on, Prince Charles met and chatted with Princess Caroline of Monaco, daughter of Prince Rainier and the former American actress Grace Kelly. After forty-five minutes the two of them had sized each other up and decided that there was no contest. They found that they simply had little in common.

But the rumors and the hopes of a liaison died hard. Later in 1977, Charles visited Canada. While there he dined and danced with Margaret Trudeau, the wife of the Prime Minister of Canada, who later left him. She was a favorite with the press and reported to anyone who was interested that she had noted Prince Charles's roving eye peering down the front of her cleavage while they were dancing. She even scolded him for ogling her décolletage, and, according to one story, he blushed.

Three months after she had separated from her husband

Margaret was in Paris and telephoned Prince Charles at Buckingham Palace. Later on she told the press that the two of them had agreed to a secret rendezvous in Paris. However, she said that the French paparazzi were driving her crazy and so she moved out of the Grand Hotel to the Manchester.

Registering herself as "Sinclair," her maiden name, she hid out for a time. When Charles phoned her at the Grand Hotel, he was not put through to her at the Manchester. No one knew at the Manchester that Sinclair was Trudeau. When Margaret finally realized her mistake in not leaving a forwarding message, she telephoned Buckingham Palace again, but, she told the press, Charles was gone.

Actually, he was at Balmoral with his family.

The rejected ex-wife flew on to the Bahamas. "When he first saw me in Ottawa," she said, "I knew I'd get him interested in me."

Every so often Prince Charles managed to get back at the press with a prankish sense of humor that dated from his school days. In March 1977, Charles had gone on a safari holiday in Kenya. The press heard that he had spent most of his time camping out with an unidentified blonde woman on a nine-day jungle jaunt.

As he was getting into his twin-engined Andover to fly out of Kenya for the African coast, he ran into a group of journalists at the airport. He grinned at them and tossed a package out to one of the *Daily Mirror* reporters.

"Here's your mystery blonde bird," he told them, and waved goodbye.

The reporters opened the package to find a stuffed pigeon with a long golden wig glued to its head. But it took a great deal to keep a reporter's imagination in check. "The hair is real," the scribe intoned as he peered at the dead pigeon. "The question is—where did *it* come from?"

That anecdote always gave Diana a giggle. She enjoyed the same puckish sense of humor he did, no question about it. In the same vein, she had been amused at what happened to Charles's attachment to Fiona Watson.

Fiona, the daughter of a Yorkshire landowner and soap king, Lord Manton, became one of Charles's escorts for a short time early in the year. She had a boyfriend, Patrick Anderson, whom she dated along with Charles.

Again it was the press that finally put an end to Fiona's courtship. In an interview, Anderson revealed to the newspapers that Fiona had appeared in an eleven-page spread in *Penthouse* magazine three years before. Sure enough, when the press grabbed up a copy, there were the eleven pages of totally unveiled Fiona in her birthday suit.

But that wasn't the kicker of the episode. Anderson also told the press that he didn't really mind the fact that Fiona was running around with the Prince of Wales. After all, she was living with *him* and always came home right after a date.

By the time the Royal Ascot Race Meeting occurred in mid-June, Charles was ready for someone else. It was to the Ascot that Charles took Lady Sarah Spencer, on one of his first dates with her. He had been taking out Lady Camilla Fane, a brunette daughter of the Earl and Countess of Westmoreland. He settled on Sarah for a time.

And it was during this courtship while on a visit to Althorp for the pheasant shoot that Diana had decided she would force her sister's hand and get the Prince of Wales to notice her. After all, they had been neighbors for sixteen years.

Although she had heard nothing from Sarah since she and Charles had spent two weeks together at Charles's chalet in Klosters, Diana assumed that the romance was progressing satisfactorily. By now she had decided that she really didn't care. If Charles was too steeped in tradition to ignore the twelve-year age gap between them, there wasn't much she could do about it.

As it was, she and Carolyn had more than one talk about Prince Charles. Not only Carolyn, but Virginia and Anne as well were interested in his romance with Diana's sister. In a way, it made him seem like one of the family.

"Diana," Carolyn said to her one evening, "have you seen this?"

"This" was a copy of *Woman's Own*, a popular magazine. "No," Diana admitted. "What's in it?"

"There's an interview with your sister." Carolyn made a face. "Don't read it. It'll curl your hair."

Diana took the magazine gingerly. Carolyn's admonition was a definite challenge. She began leafing through the story, and, indeed, it did make her eyes widen. The gist of the story was that Lady Sarah Spencer's interest in the Prince of Wales was strictly a matter of low-profile, chaste friendship.

"Our relationship," she said at one point, "is strictly platonic. I think of him as the big brother I never had."

Diana snorted when she came to that passage. "Whatever made her say anything like that?" she giggled. "Why, that's absolute nonsense. Where did they get these quotes?"

Carolyn said nothing. She was waiting for Diana to get to the end of the story.

"There is no chance of my marrying him," Lady Sarah was quoted as saying. "I'm not in love with him. And I wouldn't marry anyone I didn't love whether he were the dustman or the King of England."

Diana almost dropped the magazine. She blinked. "In a way, that does sound like our Sarah! Yet, what's the point?"

The quote continued

"If he asked me, I would turn him down."

Diana threw up her hands.

."What do you think?" Carolyn asked her. "I mean, is it the real thing?"

"Well, it certainly does *sound* like Sarah. But I don't understand why she would ever say anything like that in front of a reporter." She frowned. "Maybe it was tricked out of her."

The story set Diana to thinking. It was not like Sarah to say anything that wasn't the truth. All three Spencer girls had been brought up to tell the truth. None of them believed in telling even a little white lie. And yet. . .

Then Diana read another interview in the London *Sun*. There were more quotes from Sarah. The Charles-watchers were out in force now, trying to make or break the Charles-Sarah relationship.

"I am very fond of the Prince," Sarah said in one story. "He makes me laugh a lot. I enjoy being with him. I adore his love of horses."

Diana sniffed at that one. She went on reading about Charles, as seen through the eyes of Sarah. Sarah told about being picked up in his Aston Martin and accompanying him to one of the royal residences. She even went on at great length about the amount of wardrobe involved in going on a weekend date at Windsor Castle. It involved a suitcase full of clothes, a typical ensemble requiring a riding habit in the morning, a day dress for lunch, a skirt for tea, and a long dress for dinner. She even said that the Prince of Wales must always be addressed as "Sir," until, as might happen, he would ask you to call him "Charles." And, of course, there was always that damper on any date with him in the form of his detective who would be waiting around.

"What utter drivel," Diana exclaimed.

One weekend she called up Sarah at her South Kensington place.

"You've been talking a lot," Diana observed. "In public."

"If you're talking about that *Woman's Own* thing, I was right at home during the interview."

"Did you say all that?"

"Nothing was made up." Her voice was curious. "Why? Are you surprised?"

"It's all over?"

Sarah chuckled. "Charles was furious when the story appeared."

"I can imagine. It must have been a nasty surprise to have one of his family or friends bring him a copy of that story."

"No. I called Charles immediately after the interview. I told him exactly what I had said."

"And?"

"Let's say he was not overly pleased."

"But how do *you* feel about it?"

"Just read the interview. It's all there." Sarah was becoming abrupt.

Diana hung up thoughtfully. In a way she was not surprised. Sarah had hinted at the fact that Charles fell in love easily, and out of love as easily. Perhaps he had dropped her and she had taken out her revenge on him in public.

In a way, it was an unhappy occasion for Diana. Even though she was envious of Sarah's relationship with Charles, now that the affair had gone kaput, she would not be running into the Prince of Wales with her sister.

Of course, it was obvious that he would not drift out of the life of the Spencers completely; the family was much too close to the royal family for that. Besides, Diana's grandmother was still the Queen Mother's intimate.

Perhaps the story was a ploy. Perhaps Sarah thought that by coming out in public with her lack of concern she would force Charles into making a move. If so, Diana thought, it was the wrong tactic.

Prince Charles still took Lady Sarah out on dates, but their ardor, if it had ever been really ardor on both their parts, was quite cooled down now. They were, in the current phrase, "just friends."

4

Diana Spencer drove her blue Volkswagen through London's crowded traffic to Kensington High Street. There she turned in through the iron gates past the wrought iron railings that separated the Kensington Palace grounds from the public street and sidewalk. The security guard checked her identification, and then waved her on through.

She loved the mellowed red brick decor of Kensington Palace, which had a long and distinguished royal history. There was a feeling of pastoral calm evident in the atmosphere once she had passed through the gates, a rural feeling that was maintained purposely for the residents. Most of them worked in some capacity for the royal family.

Christopher Wren had refurbished the old mansion, originally called Nottingham House, in 1698, and since that date it had been expanded within the confined space of the estate. There was almost a feeling of a village community; Diana drove past little walled gardens and cobbled courtyards, some ablaze with flowers.

The buildings themselves were built of ancient brick, with white gables peeking out of the sloping shingled roofs, and with large multipaned sliding windows spaced along the outside walls.

Her sister Lady Jane Fellowes lived down the street from the main cluster of houses. Their residence was called The Barracks—but it was a far cry from any army barracks Diana had ever seen.

She parked the car and got out to walk up the steps. Jane came out to meet her, shading her eyes from the bright sunshine. As they walked in through the entryway, Diana could see that her sister had begun to add her own intimate touches to the furnishings, which had been utilitarian and drab at first.

The interior walls had been freshly painted in pastel tones; Jane had hung prints and oils in the various rooms. The two sisters sat in the sunny sitting room overlooking Kensington Gardens. Nannies pushed baby carriages through the formal pathways; toddlers were at play nearby. The full-leaved plane trees formed a backdrop for the scene, with the blue sky stretching above, reminiscent of a Constable landscape.

Talk drifted around to their sister Sarah. Jane said that she had seen her several days before at her home. "She seems perfectly fine," she told Diana.

"What did she say about Charles?" Diana wondered.

"Well, you know Sarah."

Yes. Sarah could be abrupt. She could also be sweet and charming and noncommittal. "Is it all over?"

"They're still good friends." Jane smiled.

"Whatever happened?"

"Only Sarah and Charles know."

"But you must have some ideas."

Jane blushed. "I don't know, of course, but—" She hesitated. "It's all speculation."

"Naturally."

"If you want my candid opinion, I think Charles is getting a bit long in the tooth to be running around with girls a lot younger than he is."

Diana was sharp. "Well, he's only twenty-nine. Is that ancient?"

"He's developing into another Uncle Edward."

Diana remembered hearing about Edward VIII; she had seen pictures of him.

"*He* didn't marry until he was over thirty. And *then* look what happened."

Diana knew. So did everyone else. Edward VIII had been forced to renounce the throne, to abdicate, in order to marry Wallis Simpson, a divorcée. And in abdicating, he had almost weakened the English throne to a point of dissolution.

"Perhaps he wants to be sure."

"Oh, he wants to be sure, that's for certain." Jane frowned. "But he's beginning to act like an aging romantic—falling in love at the drop of a hat."

"Is he *really* so susceptible?"

"I believe Sarah. He fell in love with her. She liked him. I think she was a little surprised when things fell apart."

"Maybe she misread him," Diana suggested.

"Sarah? Misread a man?" Jane stared at Diana in disbelief. "Come now. You know she's much too astute for that!"

"That ski trip to Klosters must have been the end."

"Sort of a downhill ending, that sort of thing?"

"She didn't handle him right," Diana said softly. "She should have asserted herself."

"Practicing to be a marriage broker?"

Diana laughed. "I can't help thinking about that strange interview in the magazine."

"Nor can I. Still, it's Sarah's life, you know, and not ours."

They sat in silence a moment. Then Diana said, "Whom do you think he's going to marry?"

"*I* think the best one for him—that's not saying he's going to marry her, of course—is Lady Jane Wellesley." Jane pursed her lips.

"Perhaps," Diana said absently.

Robert Fellowes came into the room at that moment, and the gossip terminated. For the time being Diana chased all thoughts of Charles and his romances out of her mind. But on the way home to Coleherne Court in the blue Volks she thought about the eighth Duke of Wellington's daughter and remembered all the stories she had heard about Prince Charles and Lady Jane.

In many ways, Jane Wellesley was one of the first of Prince Charles's "true loves" to be declared by one and all (and that included even the royal family) to be suitable as a candidate for Queen of England. Dark-haired, solidly built, and even-tempered, Lady Jane began going out with Charles in 1973, when he was still in the service.

Besides being pretty and well connected, she was an intelligent and bright girl. She had been brought up in the lifestyle of the English court, even though she was not a real member of the royal family, any more than Diana Spencer was. And Lady Jane had a cheering section inside the Palace: both the Queen and Prince Philip thought her a splendid catch for Charles.

Diana had steeped herself in the press coverage during those years. Much stress was put on Lady Jane's mischievous sense of humor and pixieish love of practical jokes—a characteristic that made her very much like Charles. But she was able to stem her own sense of the outlandish and act with complete decorum and good taste when it became necessary.

After being educated at St. Mary's Church of England Convent School in Berkshire, she went to work first in the Old Bond Street Art Gallery. She was only twenty-three when Charles started to take her out regularly. Unfortunately, she was apparently too young and too inexperienced to adjust to the constant pressure of publicity that centered on the Prince of Wales.

It was in all the newspapers when Lady Jane Wellesley and Prince Charles vacationed in Spain at Lady Jane's enormous thirty-thousand-acre estate. The land came directly down the family line from the "Iron Duke," the First Duke of Wellington, part of the spoils of his successful Peninsular Campaign of 1813. The estate, called Molino del Rey, was not far from Granada.

During a break in his duties aboard the *Minerva*, Charles retired there with Lady Jane in 1973. *Molino* means "windmill" in Spanish, and there were plenty of them in Spain, including the one Don Quixote attacked many years before; the Wellesley estate was named for one of them called the "Windmill of the King."

The estate turned out to be not quite the lonely and isolated retreat that it was supposed to be. The press found out about the outing and descended on the peninsula in full force and regalia. Oddly enough, Lady Jane had ambitions at the time to be a journalist, but had been unable to find a job on a newspaper.

Prince Charles was carrying on in his usual fashion, quite ready for the usual holiday hunt. On the first day he bagged two dozen partridge on the grounds, which included olive groves, potato fields, and grazing land. He also collected a number of newspapermen who swarmed over the fields with cameras and writing pads at the ready.

After fiercely questioning the members of the hunting party about the goings on, the press learned that Charles had hugged and kissed Lady Jane on several occasions when he should have been paying more attention to the dogs and foxes. This revelation whetted the appetite of the world of journalism, and more and more paparazzi and press types assaulted the Windmill of the King. There was such a conglomeration of them that the Guardia Civil had to be called out to quell the riotous doings, a police action that had a nasty edge to it.

There were bloody set-tos between the Spanish people and the tough government police—never a pretty sight but more brutal than usual during this episode. Charles, usually a model of cool, lost his temper and shouted out abuse and four-letter words to the people around him, a thing he simply never did.

He made up for it by apologizing for some of his language. His detective bodyguard was quoted as saying: "They are just two young people relaxing with friends for a few days. The publicity their friendship has raised has not made it easy for them."

The story was blown up out of all proportion; Diana knew the truth from people close to the royal family. The gossip columns contained notices about Lady Jane playfully pulling the Prince of Wales's hair, and throwing melons at him. It really didn't seem much like a romantic interlude at all.

In fact, Charles's detective, Paul Officer, himself spoke about any possible romance between them in these words: "I can definitely state that there is no romance. The whole affair has been built up from a molehill to a mountain. It is just not on—the two are just very good chums. The prince will not be a party to deception. That is why he has refused to be photographed with Lady Jane."

Diana and others close to Prince Charles knew the real reason he had refused to be photographed. She was truly frightened to death by all the publicity, the popping of the flash bulbs, and the yelling of questions at the two of them.

She had every right to be upset. The pressure from the media did not abate even after the two of them were back in England. During a weekend at Sandringham when Lady Jane was invited to the castle to be a guest of the royal family, the press found out about it and so did the public.

Almost ten thousand people fought their way through the gates into the public passage that wound through the estate—public property that could not be sealed off. They screamed and yelled and ogled the pair whenever they became visible. The roads in England were jammed and traffic was stopped as far back as the Midlands, almost fifty miles away.

Later on, Lady Jane had to push her way by sheer force of muscle through horrendous crowds of reporters and photographers to get from her Fulham home out to the garage and into her car to drive to work. During the day she was interrupted almost every five minutes by telephone calls asking for comments on her situation with Charles.

Even though she told the reporters nothing, she found that as soon as she got out of the office to go home at night she would be reading huge placards at every newsstand:

MY LOVE FOR CHARLES—JANE TELLS ALL

Reporters swarmed around her at the place where she worked at the Old Bond Street Art Gallery. They demanded to have news of the romance.

"There's no romance," Jane told them, almost tearfully. "We are just very good friends. It is nonsense what has been said by the press."

Diana knew the inside story about that, too. The fact was that Charles was quite definitely in love with Lady Jane. And she was in love with him. But there simply wasn't any letup in the tremendous pressure on them exerted by the media. They were never able to get away for even a few quiet moments to sort things out between themselves.

"The chemistry simply seemed to evaporate," one of Diana's friends close to the Palace told her. "Maybe they simply knew one another too well. They saw each other in 1973 and 1974, and then things cooled down."

Lady Jane felt herself surrounded by friends who had turned into enemies. She knew that she was losing a grip on her feelings. Any relationship that might have been allowed to flourish and mature into something more than a simple companionship was nipped in the bud.

"There is nothing for anyone to get excited about," she protested wearily. "This is all so ridiculous."

In 1974 when the Queen attended the Game Fair at Stratfield Saye, the home of the Duke of Wellington, even the normally patient Duke became irritated at the amount of press coverage and the magnitude of the rumors surrounding his daughter and Prince Charles. Journalists of all the various media parked on the doorstep waiting for the Prince to arrive. The Duke knew for a fact that Charles would be abroad at the time of the Game Fair and would not attend the affair even though the Queen would.

Fanning the flames of the rumors were various stories about the two "lovers." London bookies had Lady Jane as the firm favorite in the royal marriage sweepstakes. It was during this time that Charles finally told reporters in Melbourne where he was on shipboard that he had no special girl in his life.

Diana could remember the amusement of the people in the know when the French press broke its sensational story about Charles and Lady Jane shortly after that. It was a story made up out of whole cloth.

Prince Charles, the story went, had put on a false beard in order to visit his lover, Lady Jane, in the secrecy of her Fulham residence. And the French had a picture to prove it! The photograph was a doctored-up picture of Charles, to whom the Gallic art department had donated a fake beard.

The rest of the story was just as fake, with a kind of French insouciance about it. The intimate visit would have remained a secret, the newsprint went, if it had not been for a sixty-year-old woman living opposite the Fulham residence.

The newspaper quoted the woman in fractured English, and then stated with a leer that the woman was unable "to keep her tongue in her pocket."

After that, things between Charles and Jane Wellesley cooled off considerably, although he saw her regularly. Just one year before, in 1977, Prince Charles had invited Lady Jane to Balmoral Castle for a weekend. She went with him over to Scona Palace where he was playing polo and watched the game. By the time the game was over, the press was there in full strength. Someone had alerted the paparazzi to the fact that Lady Jane was present.

Diana heard that she was close to tears when she had to part from him; she had wanted to say goodbye to him properly when she had to return to London. Because of the barrage of press attention, she had to drift off all by herself.

And there was more than irony in Lady Jane Wellesley's relationship with Prince Charles. By that time, she had finally made the switch from art to journalism herself. She had joined the British Broadcasting Corporation, where she finally became deputy head of research for the weekly *Radio Times*. Soon afterward she moved to the public relations department at the BBC-TV center.

"If you can't beat the enemy," Lady Sarah had joked to Diana one night, "join them."

Eventually Lady Jane did just that, and became chairwoman of her union's branch, after which she became a member of the national executive. Even then the press continued to hound her. Was this any way to treat a fellow reporter?

Nicholas Soames, a friend of Prince Charles's whom

Diana knew, once shook his head and told her privately, "Jane is a jolly nice girl and I really pity her about the publicity."

In truth, it was the publicity that broke up her relationship with Prince Charles. Diana heard through the grapevine that she told her friends finally, "I couldn't, just couldn't, give everything up to become his wife." At another time, she blew up when someone asked her if she was going to become engaged to Prince Charles. "Do you honestly believe," she cried out, "I want to be the Queen?"

But both Diana and her sister Jane knew that Charles still dated Jane Wellesley on occasion. But, of course, so did their own sister, Lady Sarah!

It was shortly after her talk with Jane that Diana's quiet life in London was upset abruptly with a phone call from Althorp.

"It's your father," Raine told Diana in a serious voice. "He's had a massive brain hemorrhage."

Diana gripped the phone hard. "Where is he?"

"Northampton Hospital. I'm there now."

"Shall I come?"

"Please. I should like it if you could."

"I'll be there as soon as I can."

"The doctors—" Raine took a breath "—they don't know if he'll survive the night."

When Diana finally got there hours later, she found Raine arguing with one of the doctors. Diana had no idea what the discussion was about, but it was a vitriolic one. She tried to intervene, but no one paid any attention to her.

"He needs a brain clinic," Raine finally told Diana. "I can't leave him here. It's no good!"

Diana drew Raine aside. "How can we get him to London?"

"I don't know. They won't let me use a hospital ambulance." Raine's voice became determined. "I'll charter a private ambulance!"

It was a seventy-mile ride. But within hours Diana's father was admitted to one of the country's finest brain clinics, in London. Now Raine took over once again. Diana was amazed—as were her sisters and brother—at their stepmother's devotion and determination. For hours she would sit at his bedside, talking to him, trying to pull him back to life again. What he needed, of course, was the will to live.

One crisis almost immediately intervened. Raine became disenchanted with the doctor who had been assigned to Earl Spencer's case. When he told Raine that she was not helping by her infernal interfering and that he knew best, she immediately fired him and hired another.

Within a week Raine had become annoyed with the hospital accommodations. She immediately had her husband discharged and admitted to another hospital nearby to get better facilities.

Still Diana's father was in a coma, and remained in one for days. Raine kept sitting there at his side, talking constantly to him, telling him he had to reach out and grasp hold of life again. She would not stop.

Diana kept visiting whenever she could. She always found Raine there, waiting for the moment when Earl Spencer would come out of the coma.

He did so. And she continued to nag at him, trying to pull him back to life. It was a small beginning, but from that she accomplished the miracle. She made him regain his tenuous hold on life; she had confidence galore, and she gave him enough of it to force him to defy death.

It was a long, agonizing recuperation, helped along every step of the way by Raine's unflagging devotion and presence. Without her, Diana believed, her father certainly would have died.

By the autumn of 1979, Earl Spencer was cured, and the only indication that he had been gravely ill was a slight hesitation and slurring in his speech. But Diana was close to him, and perhaps she was the only one who noticed.

5

In the early summer of 1979 Diana Spencer involved herself in several short-lived jobs, and spent an enjoyable time with her mother on the island of Seil in Scotland. The weather there was much more bracing and stimulating than was the London humidity, and she loved the solitude and the peace and quiet of the remote countryside. When she wasn't spending her weekends in Scotland, she was enjoying the holidays at Althorp with her father.

Life in London was busy and suddenly productive. In the spring she had answered the telphone one day to find herself speaking with one of her old West Heath friends, Kay Seth-Smith.

After a long discussion about friends and acquaintances, Diana and Kay began talking about their future plans.

"Are you going to University?" Kay asked.

"With my grades?" Diana snorted.

"What are you doing?"

"Working here and there. I did some baby-sitting and some cooking for a caterer."

"Cooking?" Kay exclaimed.

Diana laughed. "That didn't last long."

"Victoria and I are in business together, you know. She's married—Mrs. Victoria Wilson now."

"What kind of a business is it?"

"Oh. We've opened a kindergarten in Pimlico."

Diana's interest picked up. "How is it going?"

"Very well! We're working out of an old Boy Scout building on St. George's Square." There was a hesitation. "Do I sense interest?"

"Absolutely!" Diana exclaimed.

"You're very good with children. I remember that." Kay's voice rose. "Why don't you come down and talk to us? We've got a full staff now. But in the fall when we open again, we may be able to squeeze someone else in."

Diana's "interview" was strictly a gossip session for three over tea; the proprietors of the Young England Kindergarten promised to find an opening for her for the fall semester. She would be making about four dollars an hour, but the low scale of pay didn't matter to her.

That summer her social life firmed up a bit. She met a young lieutenant in the Scots Guards and began going out with him more or less regularly. His name was Rory Scott. He had been selected in 1979 as the young officer in charge of carrying the regimental colors at the Trooping Colour ceremony. In that position he had gained exposure when he was featured prominently in a television documentry made about the Trooping.

He was twenty and enjoyed going about with Diana. In fact, Diana even did him a favor by taking his shirts back to the apartment to wash and iron. It was all very *Angry Young Man* and semidomesticated.

"Are you in love with him?" Carolyn asked her one night.

"He's a very nice young man," Diana said with a smile. "I like him because he has never tried to get serious with me."

"You don't *want* to be serious?"

"Not just yet."

It was a comfortable arrangement. With Rory taking up more and more of her off hours, she seemed to be settling into a nice routine that was stimulating and varied as well as relaxing. To Diana, life in London was very pleasant and proper. There was only one thing missing. . . .

One July afternoon Diana got a telephone call at the apartment. It was her brother-in-law, Robert Fellowes. Diana knew that Jane was expecting, and now Robert told her that Diana was a bona fide aunt. He suggested that Diana drop everything and come up to help her sister Jane cope with her first days as a mother.

"Where are you, Robert?"

"Balmoral Castle. With the royal party."

"I'll come as soon as I can."

When she hung up, Diana smiled faintly. Everyone had been waiting for the first grandchild of the eighth Earl Spencer, and somehow it was fitting that the baby should be born in the royal residence. Diana loved Balmoral. She had been there before with members of her family on special occasions.

Immediately, Diana made arrangements to fly to Aberdeen, Scotland. Then she telephoned her brother-in-law and told him when the plane would arrive. He said he would pick her up at Dyce Airport near Aberdeen. She lay down for a brief rest and rose refreshed to call a cab out to Heathrow. It was a weekday and London Airport was only mildly bustling. She boarded the British Airways Trident jet and waited for the plane to take off.

Two hours later the plane landed at Dyce without incident. There was a kind of underlying excitement in the air. Offshore oil drilling in the North Sea had brought that whole area of Scotland alive with the smell of money. Only five hundred and fourteen miles away from Heathrow, yet Aberdeen was in a different country from London.

She found her brother-in-law without effort. He carried her bags to the car and they set out for Balmoral Castle, some forty-five miles away.

"How was the flight?"

"Fine!" Diana took a deep breath. "I love it here! The air's always so much clearer!"

"Except for that smell of oil and money," he joked.

They soon left the crowded streets of Aberdeen and got on A93 traveling west into the hills. Diana could see glimpses of the River Dee as the road twisted and turned, going up into the lower reaches of Balmoral Forest. They went through Banchory, Aboyne, Ballater, and then Robert made the turnoff to the Castle of Balmoral.

"How is Jane?"

"Fine. You'll love your little niece!"

They were in the real Highlands now, almost a thousand feet above sea level. Suddenly Balmoral Castle appeared in front of them, jutting up out of the forest surrounding it like some kind of painting in a nursery book. Built of gray granite, it was designed in the traditional Scots baronial style, with one large main tower soaring a hundred feet into the air, on which was mounted the flag announcing the presence of the Queen at the castle. Several lesser rounded towers, capped by inverted cone tops, gave the castle an air of fairyland enchantment.

Balmoral had originally belonged to the Farqueharsons of Inverey, and was sold in the nineteenth century to Sir Robert Gordon, whose trustees then sold it to Albert,

Queen Victoria's consort. Since that time it had been a favorite of the royal family, particularly Queen Elizabeth and Prince Philip, who spend a great deal of time there during the year.

The castle was sited in such a fashion that it provided a spectacular view of the surrounding Scots countryside—rugged, forested, and beautiful by any standards. From the castle Diana had often looked out around her to see Ballochbuie and Braemar to the west, Glen Gairn to the north, Lochnager and the beautiful Valley of the Dee to the south.

Traditionally, the royal family spent most of the summer and fall at Balmoral, shooting grouse, fishing for salmon, and attending the regular events associated with the area, the most important of which was the Highland Games at Braemar.

With Robert at her side, Diana paused on the threshold of the castle to look up once again at the marvelous old granite façade, the blue sky beyond, and the tiny white clouds that always seemed to be floating about, even in late summer. It was warm, but not in any way overpoweringly stuffy.

Diana quickly fell into the rhythm of the royal household, visiting with Jane and her brand-new baby girl, chatting with friends among the weekend guests, and enjoying herself immensely.

She was walking away from her sister and the baby girl to her own room later that day when she heard someone calling her name.

"Hello, Diana."

She turned quickly. Yes. It was Charles. The crooked grin, the blue eyes so bright against the suntanned face. The ingratiating way of addressing her made her heart skip a beat, just as described in the romances.

"Hello."

"How does it feel to be an Old Maid Aunt?"

They were walking along the corridor together. He was beside her. She could *feel* his presence. There was a tension in him, a masculinity that quite overcame her. Odd, he never seemed that way in public.

Still, she knew he was dating another favorite now, Anna Wallace. The gossip columns were full of the two of them. Was it on? Was it off? Looking at him, she saw that he did not appear to be thinking of anything but her at that moment.

"I love children," she said.

"Yes. You'll be working with kindergarteners soon, won't you?"

Where on earth did he learn that? she wondered. He sounded as if he had been briefed and was talking to one of his subjects. She felt a chill of disappointment.

"I'm a career girl." She closed up.

He sensed the immediate negative reaction. It seemed to puzzle him. He said nothing, but studied her as she walked along beside him. She felt his gaze intimately. There were all kinds of odd things going on inside her. She stiffened purposely.

"Here's my room," she said, turning to face him.

He stood there, inches from her. The blue eyes were watching her face for some sign. She determined to give him no sign. After a moment he wheeled and went on down the corridor. "We'll talk later," he said over his shoulder, with a typically royal wave.

Frustrated, she pushed open her door and slammed it shut behind her. Boiling, she sat on the bed and smashed her fist into the counterpane. She was furious, but she had no idea whether she was angry at herself for not making more of an opportunity with Charles, or furious at him for not making more of an opportunity with her.

She stalked over to the window and looked out. Almost immediately the grandeur of the scene—the Highlands spread out almost to the sea in front of her—alleviated the fury that was eating at her. She began breathing more evenly. The scene was so beautiful and so spectacular that she found the tears coming to her eyes.

Well, she thought stoically, there was nothing wrong with crying about a beautiful landscape, was there? And she let the tears roll down her cheeks.

What was the matter with her?

Charles was true to his promise. Several days later he found her near the fireplace at night, staring down into the flames. She had spent a marvelous day with her sister and the baby. Then she had gone for a rambling walk in the woods around the castle. She still smelled the scent of pine. The clean bright air had cleansed her soul. She was scheduled to leave in a few days. It would be a wrench, leaving the Scots soil she loved so much.

"It takes the edge off the chill," a voice said near her. "The fire, I mean."

She smiled. She had not seen Charles since the episode in the corridor. He had been hunting and riding around the country for visits to the small villages. Part of his job, as he liked to put it.

"I've been practicing that dance step you taught me—where was it?—at Sandringham?"

"On the terrace," Diana recalled. "Well? Are you going to audition for the BBC?"

"As a stand-up comedian?" He looked startled.

She was giggling. "I forgot you'd done some stage work."

"I was a super Macbeth, I'll have you know. Thane of Cawdor, no less."

There was a short silence. Diana realized that it was a comfortable one, not the uneasy kind that made her want to jump in and say something before everything came crashing down.

"Is London treating you well?"

"I love it."

"The swinging life?"

"Oh, I date fairly regularly." She was smiling.

"That's what I was curious about. Your love life."

She shrugged. "I know one very nice young man."

"I should hope so." The grin returned. "I'm referring to the 'one' in the statement and not the 'nice'."

"You can stress the 'nice' too, if you wish," Diana came back.

"London seems to have changed since the last time I was there."

"When was that?"

"A week ago."

"It hasn't changed. And I haven't, either." She felt herself blushing nicely.

Another silence. Comfortable. Easy.

"Sorry I've been so busy this time around. Look, perhaps you'd like to go for salmon tomorrow morning."

"I'm afraid not. My schedule is much too tight." She wasn't looking at him. She had no idea why she was turning him down. It didn't make sense.

He seemed honestly disappointed. "Maybe next time."

"Of course," she said lightly. She was cursing herself for not promising to go no matter what, but then decided that she would sound too gauche. Best to conform to her image—the steady, decent, regular career girl.

Someone called Charles from the other end of the room, and he excused himself and left. She did not see him again on that visit to Balmoral. Shortly after this second brief conversation with him, news came over the telephone that Charles's great uncle, Lord Louis Mountbatten, of all his relatives *the* favorite, had been assassinated by Irish Republican Army terrorists while vacationing on the west coast of Ireland.

A pall was immediately cast over the royal party. Diana

was shattered to find members of the family, usually so stiff-upper-lipped and phlegmatic, openly weeping in the corridors and drawing rooms. Diana cut short her visit to her sister and took the plane back to London.

In the fall she began working at the Young England Kindergarten, and stayed through a brief trial period. She liked the work. Her friends who ran the school liked the way she got along with the children. She stayed on, more or less on a regular part-time basis, and thrived at the work.

She tried to put Prince Charles out of her mind, and succeeded fairly well. After all, she was reading about him in the newspapers—about his romance with Anna Wallace mostly—and she knew she must consider him objectively and simply as the next heir to the throne. Well, she *tried* to put him out of her mind, but she really couldn't.

In the dead of winter, a bitterly cold February weekend, she was invited by the Queen to Sandringham for a brief stay. Ostensibly, she was to be the companion of Prince Andrew, who was spending a few days home. She enjoyed herself when she was with him, as she always had. He was a jovial companion. He liked to charm the women. Diana had never really felt anything for him except a kind of next-door friendship because of their early days together.

Prince Charles was present, but he kept to himself, exchanging only a few words with her. For the most part, he busied himself with obligations and with the shoot. Diana thought he seemed a bit irritable and moody, but it might have been her imagination. On the outside he was the same. A difficult man to diagnose, she thought—most difficult.

She returned to London after an exciting weekend, exhausted. She went to bed early after gorging herself on chocolate cake, Twiglets, and ginger biscuits, the medicine with which she regularly fortified herself to stroke up her system.

She finished up her term at the kindergarten and in July

1980 she was astonished to find herself invited to the polo match at Cowdray in Sussex. Prince Charles was playing for Les Diables Bleus. She went, even though watching someone else playing a game on a horse a quarter of a mile away from the stands wasn't exactly her idea of a romantic date.

There were a great many of Charles's polo-playing friends about, and it was a noisy encounter at best. There were so many together that she felt pretty much like one in a cast of thousands. In fact, she couldn't really remember whether the Blue Devils won or lost.

But the best thing about the polo match fiasco was the fact that Charles asked her to make sure to attend the Cowes Regatta two weeks later. She would be expected aboard the royal yacht *Britannia* all during Cowes Week in August. Cowes Week was similar to the Royal Ascot in mid-June.

There was another huge crowd aboard the royal yacht. Charles's polo-playing buddies seemed like a tiny and well-disciplined group compared to the mobs on the yacht. The Regatta was always held on the Isle of Wight just south of London. When they began, the races and festivities were exciting and stimulating; at the end they wound down into something less than that.

Charles finally got onto a sailboard and began sailing up and down, past the royal yacht in The Solent. The Solent is the narrow strait of ice-cold water flowing between the Isle of Wight and the coast of Hampshire. The sailboard was a one-man craft with a sail, a mast, and a small hull.

Diana was unable to resist temptation. As Prince Charles came by, grinning at everyone on the deck of the royal yacht, clowning about and acting the fool, she felt one of her impish moments surfacing. This time, she could not squelch it. She leaned out over the rail as he went sailing by for the tenth time, grabbed at the mast, flung it to one side, and sent the skipper tumbling into The Solent.

Prince Charles unceremoniously and ignominiously met the ice-cold current of The Solent face first, with his eyes wide open and his mouth agape. He vanished from sight, with Diana and her astonished companions watching him.

Spluttering and coughing, Charles came out of the water gazing in astonishment at the group standing at the railing grinning down at him. He thrashed himself over to the overturned sailboard and righted it quickly. He looked up at the laughing faces again, his own face red, and carefully studied the expressions there. He saw Diana. Diana knew he saw her.

Holding her breath, she waited for him to blow up. For a long moment he held his rage, waiting to loosen it. Then, quite suddenly, he turned and sailed away. Diana was blushing. She wondered again why she had done such a foolish thing. The little imp inside her had probably ruined any chance she might have of being one of Charles's real friends now.

"Goodbye, sweet prince," she thought to herself. Everyone around her was amused and congratulated her on her sense of fun and daring. Oh sure, she thought. Very daunting, I'm sure.

6

Prince Charles came away from his dunking in The Solent with any male's annoyance and pique at being made to look a fool. At first he did not connect any one of the many laughing faces behind the rail of the royal yacht with his particular tormentor. In fact, he simply didn't care. He had too many other things to worry about to waste time on avenging a simple-minded trick like that.

Soon afterward, however, as he sat in his office at Buckingham Palace, going over his daily reports, he suddenly realized in an instant flash who it was. Of course, he thought; it had to be! He recalled those fumbling and stumbling moments on the great terrace at Sandringham when he was being teased into trying out some new tap dance step; he remembered chatting haltingly with her the awful week his great uncle had been killed; he remembered the crush at the polo match when everything had gone wrong and he really hadn't had a chance to talk to her.

It had to be Diana Spencer. She was the only one with enough cheek and gumption to do a thing like that to him!

But somehow she appeared to be an almost entirely different Diana Spencer. His first recollection of the Spencer girl was her appearance at the pheasant shoot at Althorp at least three years before. Then she had appeared to be an attractive, cuddly, bumptious teenager with most of the drawbacks any teenager had. But now . . .

Charles tried to picture her as she had appeared at Althorp—a now strikingly beautiful teenager with shoulder-length hair, happy and healthy, but not what anyone who was even half a connoisseur would call a "beautiful" or even "pretty" young woman.

She had even then displayed a sunny, almost indestructible disposition, and a cheerful, beaming attitude about life. She may have tended to giggles, but seemed always ready to be a pal to a man, or even something a bit more intimate.

Somewhere along the line, between then and now, that angular, almost clumsy-looking figure had vanished, and in its place now was a stately, shapely, robust woman. Her face—that was what confounded Charles. The strong English features had softened and taken on a kind of serene beauty. Her complexion was beautiful; with a peaches-and-cream texture. Her hair, which he remembered as thick and brown, now shone like burnished gold in certain sunlight—particularly the sunlight from behind her as she leaned over the deck to laugh at him. Her eyes, blue and clear and large, were steady and cool, and full of mischievous humor.

She had changed, into a smashing, attractive young woman! She was nineteen—he guessed that was about right—but she had the maturity and poise of a much more experienced woman. It was hard to believe that the sixteen year old who had talked to him at Earl Spencer's pheasant shoot and then taught him the tap dance step in her awkward, embarrassed way was now a splendidly got-out woman with none of the impishness or fun left out.

Thinking of Diana made him think of her older sister, Sarah. It was a memory that had unpleasant associations, to say the least. He had still not recovered from what he considered to be a very low blow by Lady Sarah—that interview in *Woman's Own* written by James Whitaker. It had been a long time ago, but it still upset him.

Of course, it had been easy for him to reply by phasing out his romantic attachment to her step by step. Without making the break obvious, he had shown her that it was all over for both of them. The conclusion of that relationship had been painful for him.

Had it been as painful for her? Could Diana, her sister, be trying to even it up by her treatment of him in The Solent?

In rising irritation he dismissed the thought of Lady Diana Spencer. He had work to do. Yet, of course, there was always the ongoing problem of marriage. He realized that he was over thirty and still not married. He knew that some people were even questioning his masculinity; they could hardly be aware of his private life. He certainly did not stint on the society of women. He doted on beautiful girls. But the fact remained that he was still not married.

Yet he simply could not meet a girl and fall in love with her and marry her in any sensible, normal fashion. For him, the selection of *the* girl had to be exactly right. And *right* meant much more than simply a non-Catholic, a non-divorcée, and someone approved by the Queen. *Right* meant, quite frankly, a virgin. His mother had made that quite clear to him years before. Not only must she be a virgin, but she must be publicly accepted as a virgin.

Historically, such a stipulation might have been warranted in the nineteenth century. In the swinging sixties and seventies, given the social order and the popular life-style among young men and women, the idea was absolutely laughable. In fact, for a young woman to be accepted publicly as a virgin was almost an insult; at least it was an anachronism. Nevertheless, Charles knew the feelings of his mother. The bride must be *intacta*, as the members of the medical fraternity put it.

The truth of the matter was that there simply weren't a lot of nineteen- or twenty-year-old virgins around anymore. What made it worse was his mother's insistence that he find and marry the right girl—and marry her as soon as possible. Charles knew why. The English monarchy, which had barely survived the abdication of Edward VIII, his uncle—"for the woman I love"—could not survive another crisis within so few years.

He had discussed his dilemma aloud and had been quoted in print about his marriage thoughts. "It's awfully difficult," he had said at one time, "because you've got to remember that when you marry, in my position, you're going to marry somebody who perhaps one day is going to become queen. So you've got to choose very carefully.

"The one advantage about marrying a princess, for instance, or somebody from a royal family, is that they do know what happens. The trouble is that I often feel I would like to marry somebody English. Or Welsh . . . well, British, anyway."

As for his social life, Prince Charles was a very slow starter. His position as heir apparent made it impossible for him to associate on a romantic level with his peers without causing considerable commotion. Besides that, most of his time up to his college years had been spent at predominantly male-oriented schools.

When he had enrolled at Timbertop, a private school in Australia, he had exchanged letters with Rosaleen, the daughter of a retired major named John Bagge who lived near Sandringham. When Charles returned to Gordons-toun, in Scotland, he continued to write her.

Charles-watching had become an established custom in Fleet Street. Almost every week there was a story about him, even when nothing was going on. An enterprising journalist found the correspondence. It was published. Charles remembered the incident with a pang.

Because of publication of the letters, the Bagge family was subjected to all kinds of embarrassment. On one occasion, when members of the royal family encountered the Bagges at a formal affair, they gave them the cold stare of monarchy, making the Bagges shrivel into the ground. Charles had simply curled up with shame and indignation. The friendship had immediately terminated.

At Cambridge, things were different. He dated Cindy Buxton, the daughter of Aubrey Buxton, a television executive and family friend from East Anglia. Charles knew Cindy socially anyway. But the press examined his behavior through a magnifying glass. Then, when nothing happened, some of the scribes made up stories that he was spending more time trying to kiss Cindy than dance with her at a local ball.

It was Lucia Santa Cruz, the daughter of the Chilean Ambassador to London, who was his first. She was working for the Master of Trinity, Lord R. A. Butler of Saffron-Walden. Americans would call him the Dean of the College. Lucia was helping Lord Butler write up his political memoirs, acting as his research assistant.

A history graduate, she was four years older than Charles. As he found out, she had, as the saying went, been around. But she was intelligent, vivacious, and sophisticated. And she was well connected. Unfortunately, even during the swinging sixties, the Iron Curtain of Morality slammed down at curfew time each night at Cambridge, forcing students and girl friends to part.

Prince Charles, however, was a special case. Lord Butler came to his aid, declaring himself at his disposal every evening for forty-five minutes, if Charles needed him for consultation or discussion. Charles thought the approach was definitely amusing and in good taste. It was the academic way of letting him use the office. In fact, Lord Butler gave him a key to the side entrance to the Master's Lodge (the office) for his own private use.

Charles urged Lord Butler to give Lucia a duplicate key. He did so, a request, as he later said, "we were very glad to accede to."

Charles invited her for a weekend at Balmoral Castle and took her out on other dates in London, all of which caused columns of newsprint to appear about their "romance." The press set up special Charles Watches for his "weekends at Balmoral." The tabloids kept score of his current flames from that day on.

Deep in reminiscence at his desk, Charles sighed aloud. Lucia was now married to a Chilean lawyer and had several children, the first of whom was a godson of Prince Charles.

After Lucia came Sybilla Dorman, the daughter of Sir Maurice Dorman, the governor-general of Malta. A country gentleman, he owned an impressive manor house seventy miles west of London. Sybilla was reading history, just as Lucia had been doing; Charles was also doing his history at the time. Sybilla also liked dramatics, one of Charles's favorite subjects.

Charles had the use of a beat-up Land Rover which he had scrounged up from Sandringham. The first night he dated her at Cambridge he picked her up in it, driving up in triumph to her door.

"I'd expected the MG, at the very least," she told him with a pout.

Charles laughed; it was no put-on. Sybilla was apparently not teasing him. Nevertheless, they got along fine. For a time.

One night she gave a party at her college, Newnham, which lasted into the wee hours of morning, far past college curfew. The guests were forced to depart by climbing over the walls of the college. No punishment was meted out.

His best time with Sybilla occurred on the two holidays he spent with her on Malta. The journalists and photographers were as thick as flies trying to track them down. The big event of the entire holiday was a shot the paparazzi got of Sybilla rubbing suntan oil over Prince Charles's back.

When he was twenty-one, Charles was given a huge party at Buckingham Palace. Everyone was there to celebrate his coming of age. The Prince of Wales danced well into the early morning hours, and soon left with Lady Leonora Grosvenor, the daughter of the Duke and Duchess of Westminster. Lady Leonora was a dark-haired beauty who appealed to him immensely. He had finally learned to pilot a plane during his Cambridge days; he flew her that morning to Westminster, out near Chester, some one hundred sixty miles northwest of London.

The estate was a huge expanse of land including two hamlets, a golf course, two rivers, and a church. Charles had been there before for a weekend of shooting. When the papers came out with the story of his early-morning flight with Lady Leonora, the Palace was not amused. The Queen's press secretary issued a statement:

"Oh, dear, oh, dear. If they are going to read romance into it every time Prince Charles goes out with a friend, that is what we must expect."

Charles laughed in memory of all that. Lady Leonora was now married to the Earl of Lichfield, more popularly known in professional circles as Patrick Lichfield, the photographer.

Being in the armed services had cut down on Charles's social time, but it had not limited the number of women he took out. In 1970 he was running around with the twenty-year-old daughter of Lord Balniel, Bettina Lindsay. A bouncy blonde and a direct descendant of King Charles II and Nell Gwynne, Bettina was into acting, and attended a Parisian mime school. Later she became a teacher of drama. And where was Bettina now? She was Mrs. Peter Drummond-Hay.

Charles frowned. Who was next? Georgina Russell, the daughter of Sir John Russell, a career diplomat and former British Ambassador to Brazil. Here was one who could outtalk anyone! She could speak six foreign languages fluently: Russian, Portuguese, French, German, Greek, and Italian. She had a job with *Vogue*. Charles met her at Arundel, the historic home of the Duke of Norfolk.

That relationship was an embarrassment, Charles remembered with rue. Sir John and Lady Russell had reported that there would soon be an announcement of an engagement. It never came. Now Georgiana was married to a Welsh landowner, Brooke Boothby.

The Prince of Wales stood up and began pacing back and forth in his office. There was no sense in going over all his affairs of the past. Frowning, he stood staring out the window down into The Mall. What had ever prompted him into his nostalgic stroll through Memory Lane? The Spencer girl?

Of course not. Charles knew very well what had prompted him to muse on the foibles of women. He had deliberately tried to wipe her out of his mind, but was unable to do so. After the debacle with Lady Sarah Spencer, he had drifted from one relationship to another, the most memorable, and at the same time the most impossible, that with Anna Wallace.

Anna was the daughter of a millionaire, Hamish Wallace. He owned houses and estates in England and in Scotland. He had a townhouse in Mayfair. She was a slim, independent, vivacious woman. She appeared with Charles at hunts and at social affairs, usually in the country but sometimes in the city.

She lived in a small apartment off Sloane Square in exclusive Chelsea. It was there that she entertained Charles.

"You're not the first, you know," she had told him in characteristic bluntness almost of their first date.

"Oh?" Charles appeared unconcerned.

"I've had two lovers, dearest." She threw back her head and laughed. "But in three years. You can't call me fickle."

Her pedigree was excellent. She was fun to be with. Charles found himself slipping into an easygoing relationship with her. He wanted to dominate his women; but he didn't want his women to be spineless. He liked Anna's spunk.

Most of his friends liked her. "She's the most interesting woman you've brought around here," one of them told him.

Almost from the beginning, Anna showed signs of rebellion at Charles's lifestyle. She peered through the curtains of her apartment window at a car parked opposite one night. "Who's that down there in the car?"

Charles joined her at the window. "My bodyguard. Special Branch man."

"Tell him to buzz off," snapped Anna. "I don't like being tailed by detectives."

"It's all part of noblesse oblige," Charles said with a smile.

"You know what you can do with your noblesse oblige," Anna said. "Can you get rid of him?"

"I don't like being blown up by bombs," Charles retorted. "Odd as it may sound, I need him."

"Then you don't need me," snapped Anna.

"Come on, Anna love," he pleaded. "Don't be that way. I think I'm in love with you."

"Then why do you treat me like a piece of luggage?"

Most of his friends found her entrancing. Not so two people who were most important to Charles: Camilla Parker-Bowles and Lady Dale Tryon. Charles had known Camilla for years, dating back to the early 1970s. He had known Kanga, Lady Dale Tryon, for a shorter period.

Camilla was married to Andrew Parker-Bowles, a close friend of Charles's, now Household Cavalry Officer at the Palace. The Parker-Bowleses lived in Allington near Chippenham in Wiltshire; Charles was a frequent guest in their home. The two men had met at the time Andrew was escorting Camilla and Lady Caroline Percy; it was Charles who was associated with Lady Caroline for a brief period.

Camilla was a dark-haired, petite, and perceptive woman, who had been a good and steady friend of Prince Charles ever since they met. She was now a trusted confidante; he frequently sought advice from her about his amours.

Aware of Charles's deeper sensitivities and able to understand more about him and his relationships with women than he did, she always gave him excellent advice on those he was dating. Although Charles did not consider her a sounding board, he did discuss intimate details about his love life with her—facts that would have been embarrassing to the women involved. But Camilla knew how to keep her mouth shut; it was the reason for their long and affectionate friendship.

Lady Dale Tryon was the wife of Lord Anthony Tryon, son of the Queen's late treasurer. Lord Anthony was director of the merchant bankers Lazard Brothers. It was Lord Tryon who frequently gave Charles financial advice on his investments. Like Andrew Parker-Bowles, Anthony Tryon was another of Charles's hunting companions. He spent weekends on pheasant shoots with the Tryons on their seven-hundred-acre estate in Wiltshire and more extended holidays in Iceland near Egilsstadir for the best salmon fishing ever.

"Kanga" stood for "Kangaroo"—Lady Dale was born in Australia. One of Charles's friends described her once as "not a beauty in the true sense of the word, but she attracts men easily. Dustmen whistle at her, so do schoolboys. And she loves it."

In her younger days, she had a large following. The story went around that when she took a streetcar to school, there would be a crowd of boys waiting for her, just for the pleasure of seeing her and maybe sitting next to her on the way.

Unhappily for Charles, both Camilla and Kanga took exception to Anna Wallace. Usually they were quite easygoing about his many girlfriends. But for some reason he found them immediately antagonistic toward her. He found out their feelings fairly quickly. When Anna had expressed annoyance at Charles's rather strictured lifestyle, he began taking her around to see his obviously nonstrictured friends. She was fun, she was pretty, she was with it; he found that most of them took to her immediately.

Except for Camilla and Kanga. And they were the two important ones. Neither of them could tell him exactly why they disliked her. Charles became exasperated at their evasions.

"Why don't you like her?" Charles once asked Camilla.

"I don't think she's right for you," Camilla observed coolly.

"That's no answer!"

"But that's the way I feel," Camilla said serenely.

Charles tackled Kanga. "You don't like her, do you?"

"I've liked others of your friends better," said Kanga.

"What's wrong with her?"

"That's not for me to say, " Kanga retorted. "What I feel doesn't matter anyway. It's what you feel."

"I feel like I'm being evaded!"

By now Charles knew he was in love. Yet the relationship with Anna was not pursuing a smooth course at all. Anna was upset over Charles's dependence on Kanga and Camilla, who she felt were her sworn enemies.

"Why do you put so much faith in them?" she asked him.

"I like them. They're my dearest friends."

"Why?"

"Kanga makes me laugh. So does Camilla."

"Perhaps you need a court jester," snapped Anna. "Not me."

Charles tried to calm her down.

"What will happen to us?" Anna asked. "If it comes to a choice between those two or me—who will you pick?"

"You, of course."

That didn't satisfy Anna.

When the end came, the curtain fell with a dreadful clatter. Charles and Anna had been invited to a ball given by Lord Vestey. Mark Vestey had married Rosie Clifton, one of Charles's old girlfriends. Charles was in fine form that night, dancing with dozens and dozens of the guests. He knew Anna could take care of herself, and he always danced the last dance with her anyway.

It was his obligation to spend as much time as he could with the female members of the ball. He came up to Anna for the last dance—the best one of them all, as he had told her.

To his surprise he found her fuming. Her face was almost red with anger. She seemed to be trembling. Seeing the battle flags flying in her eyes, Charles nevertheless walked right up and smiled at her. "It's time for our dance."

"Why now?" Her voice rose. "Why now? You've left me alone all night!"

"I was only dancing with friends," Charles said, abashed at her unleashed anger.

"Then you don't need me!" she screamed at him, her rage breaking loose. "Now you will have to do without me!"

Anna swirled out of the ballroom through the crowds of startled guests. Charles stood in the middle of the dance floor, staring after her. Quickly he gathered his wits about him and followed her. A path opened up for him. He could not catch her. She had gone out and disappeared.

Even though she was Charles's date, she had come by herself, as was customary. She drove herself home and that was the end of Anna Wallace.

Charles was crushed. He sought advice from Kanga and Camilla. "What should I do?"

"Have you called her?" Kanga asked.

"She won't return my calls."

Camilla was more philosophical. "Perhaps it's for the best."

"Why is it for the best?" Charles asked her. "I love her."

"Well, it seems that she doesn't love you," Camilla observed quietly.

The final blow was struck on August 12, 1980. Charles was leafing through the morning *London Times* and he stopped short. There was a notice of the engagement of Anna Wallace to John Hesketh, the youngest brother of an English peer, Lord Hesketh.

Charles couldn't believe it. But, at the same time, he knew it was true. He had been definitely rejected by Anna Wallace. He was moody and depressed for days. But the episode forced him to review his lifestyle, and especially his relationship with women.

He had been playing the field for too long. He was getting just a bit old for that sort of game. All his friends were married; at least, most of them were. Most of the women he had been going with were now married, too. Something had to be done.

Something. What?

And from somewhere came the memory of a fresh face he had just seen again. Diana Spencer. Perhaps. . . .

Within days of his humiliation, Charles was dining with the Parker-Bowleses at their lovely Wiltshire home. After dinner, as they sat around the fire companionably, Charles leaned back and closed his eyes briefly.

"Now tell me please all about Diana Spencer."

Camilla sneaked a glance at Andrew; his face was a blank. "What about her? Her background? Her genealogy? What she's like?"

"I know what she's like. She's an imp." Charles opened his eyes and leaned forward. "She gave me a bad time at the Cowes Regatta."

Camilla burst out laughing. "Oh yes. That free bath in The Solent."

The Parker-Bowleses laughed together. So, finally, did Charles. He realized it was all over the country that she had ducked him.

"Serves you right," Camilla said. "I always thought those sailboards were for little boys."

"The obvious point is that Diana is Sarah Spencer's sister," Parker-Bowles said.

"I know that." Charles was irritable. He wanted answers. "Why does she keep showing up?"

"Are you interested?" Camilla asked bluntly, ignoring the question.

Charles sat up in his chair and studied his confidante carefully. "Then you assume it's no surprise that she's been appearing regularly wherever I am."

Silence.

"I'd almost think someone was pulling strings," Charles mused. "The Queen Mum? Lady Fermoy? Earl Spencer?"

"Oh, I don't think there's any kind of *plot* on," Parker-Bowles said easily.

"Are you interested?" Camilla repeated.

"Obviously he's interested," Parker-Bowles chuckled. "Or he wouldn't be asking."

"With whom is she dating? That's what you want to know, isn't it?" Camilla mused.

Charles did not dignify the question with an answer. His expression was enough.

"No one, seriously," Camilla said. "She's not a swinger. And Charles, I ought to warn you. She's just a child."

Charles flared up. "And I'm the Ancient Mariner?"

"Oh, come off it!" Parker-Bowles laughed. And they began talking hunting and shooting.

7

One evening in very early September, Lady Diana Spencer was sitting in the Coleherne Court apartment staring into space and thinking it was time to have her hair done in some different, dramaic way. The telephone rang and Carolyn, who was sitting nearest it, answered.

"Three-seven-three, seven-four-six-two," she said in an approximation of a trained secretary's tones.

She listened for a moment and there was a peculiar expression on her face. She turned to Diana. In fact, she was unable to speak for a moment. There was a slight smile on her lips when she finally got her tongue and held out the phone.

"It's for you, Diana."

"Who is it?"

"Some man who says he's from Buckingham Palace. Obviously it's one of your witty friends."

Diana laughed and took the receiver. "Hello!"

It was indeed a man. He was speaking for the Queen at the Palace. Diana Spencer had been invited to go to Balmoral Castle for the weekend coming—that would be September fifth to sixth. Would she be expected?

"Yes, I shall be there," Diana said softly.

Good. In that case, she would be met at Dyce Airport by a special envoy in the Queen's service. He would be identified by his green waterproof anorak and tweed suit. In any event he would make himself known to her; she did not have to search him out.

"Thank you," said Diana in a kind of daze. She was thinking ahead and putting a label on the invitation: she would be one of the Balmoral Weekend Girls!

Anne and Virginia had come into the room and stood looking at their apartment mate.

"Well?" Carolyn said immediately. "What's it all about?"

"I'm going to Balmoral for the weekend," she said with a wide smile.

"As a guest of Prince Charles?" cried Carolyn.

"As a guest of the Queen," Diana said steadily.

"But you can see Charles's fine Italian hand in that, can't you?"

"Oh, the Queen always makes the guest list out," Diana explained softly.

The young women all burst out laughing.

"Now you'll be one of Charles's September guests!" Anne observed excitedly.

"You're joining a long and elite list!" Virginia told her shortly.

"Who's he going with now?" Anne wondered.

"Ever since he broke up with Anna Wallace, no one," said Carolyn, who kept up on that kind of thing. "Maybe you're the heiress apparent."

"Fat chance," said Diana. "I'm one of those fill-ins between regulars."

But her eyes were starry as she began to plan her wardrobe. Within minutes she had the rest of them helping.
That meant she would have to go to her favorite store,
Harrods, next day and buy several pieces. She would need
boots, pants, sweaters, plus some decent evening clothes.

Two days later Diana called a cab and drove out to
Heathrow, lined up to board the British Airways flight
once again to Aberdeen, as she had boarded it dozens of
times in the past—but never for *this* kind of date at Balmoral.

She passed by a small group of rather seedily dressed,
hawkeyed, alert men standing against the wall with papers
and notes in their hands. Close by their feet a passel of
cameras and flash bulbs had been slung as they waited.
They were newsmen, journalists from Fleet Street.

This was the skeleton crew that always stood by to check
out the weekend manifest for Aberdeen. Everyone knew
that Charles was now in residence at Balmoral. The
Charles-watchers were always on the lookout for new girl
friends. With the Anna Wallace breakup now history, they
knew he would soon be changing the guard again.

D. Spencer, one of the newsmen noted, checking off the
manifest he had secured from the cooperative ticket checker
as she had passed through the security checkpoint. He
shrugged. A pretty girl, but a bit tall for Prince Charles. It
was not D. Spencer they were interested in; it was
D. Sheffield. Davina had been one of Charles's dates fairly
frequently.

Two hours later the man Diana expected, in the anorak
and tweed suit, gathered her up at Dyce Airport, and led
her to a special parking place where a green Range Rover
was parked. He was a quiet, unassuming young man in his
twenties, fully armed with a loaded .38-caliber revolver in a
leather holster kept well out of sight. A handpicked guard
from Scotland Yard's Special Branch, he was one of two

dozen Royal Detectives always on duty to protect the top ten members of the British Royal Family.

After the long ride up to the castle, Diana Spencer stepped out at the front entrance to the castle and hurried inside.

The guest list for the weekend at Balmoral was always extensive. Diana found that she knew quite a few of them. She had met Nicholas Soames before. He was the son of Lord Soames, who had been British Ambassador to Paris. Nicholas was the grandson of Winston Churchill. He had acted as Charles's equerry during the early 1970s, but had resigned to go into the world of finance. Now he had become one of the Prince of Wales's financial advisors, particularly on his holdings in the Duchy of Cornwall.

Soames was still a bachelor; Diana had liked him immediately on meeting him.

Another friend of Charles's at the castle was Andrew Parker-Bowles, who she had met recently. He was there without his wife Camilla, whom Diana also knew.

And there were dozens of others.

Dinner that evening in the elegant, old-fashioned state dining room was a glittering, memorable, and exclusive affair—in spite of the crowd. Under the tattered and bloodstained battle flags from long-ago wars, the weekend guests sat at the long table amid the splendor of bygone eras.

Diana was no stranger to any of the royal family intimates, although she knew some members better than others. Gone were the days now when she addressed the Queen as "Aunt Lilibet." She had called her that as a child.

The Queen was present, as was Prince Philip. So was the Queen Mother, whom everyone in the family called the "Queen Mum"—George VI's Queen who was spry and bright at eighty. And there was Prince Edward. Prince Andrew, whom Diana knew probably better than either Edward or Charles, was away in the service.

Yet, in spite of the exalted atmosphere in which she was dining, she felt relaxed and quite at home. The Queen was most enjoyable when she was out of the limelight and in the intimacy of her own family. Although most reserved and proper outside the royal residences, inside them she was a great deal of fun, with a sense of humor not unlike Prince Charles's. She had a remarkable ability to mimic people; Diana thought she knew where Charles got his histrionic talent.

The Duke of Edinburgh was a no-nonsense man, extremely masculine in appearance and bearing, but affable and charming when he wanted to be. In the heart of the family, Diana sensed that he was definitely the head and leader. Politically, of course, the Queen was the sovereign who ruled the realm; but in the confines of the royal residence it was Prince Philip who was the center of the entire group.

The Queen Mum, to whom Diana felt very close because of her grandmother's tie with her, was quiet and reserved, but she had no compunction about joining in the fun when the conversation became general. Prince Edward, sixteen and still going to Gordonstoun School in Scotland, had a sense of decorum and knew how to hold his tongue except when he wanted to loosen it. He was bright and quite outgoing usually; he was a very good student and even had a surprisingly high academic standing. Once he was finished, he would take his own turn in the armed services.

Diana had been seated directly across the table from Prince Charles, who appeared smiling and full of charm. There was none of the stiffness evident in his public appearances. In the heart of the family, he was cool, amusing, and somewhat sardonic in manner. It was a role he could play well, and one which he seemed to enjoy.

He was interested in her work with her kindergarteners, and she did her best to entertain him without telling too many anecdotes that might make her work seem ridiculous. He also questioned her about how she liked living in London; she loved that, of course, and said so.

Sitting there with the excellently liveried servants dressed in scarlet jackets as they brought in course after course on silver plates and served the food quietly and graciously, Diana had to pinch herself to be assured that she was not in a dreamworld. Of course, she *was* in a dreamworld, but she was not dreaming. Being at the absolute pinnacle of international society was a heady, almost unnerving experience, but she was being treated exactly as if she had been there all her life.

As she ate the very plain English fare—roast meat and vegetables—she heard the conversation turn to hunting and fishing. The Queen, of course, loved to fish, as did the Queen Mother. Prince Philip and Charles loved to hunt and shoot. But the two men were also good anglers. Diana did not like to hunt or shoot. Eventually she even said so.

"But of course," recalled Prince Philip. "Your father once told me you had a bad fall as a child."

"Yes," Diana admitted. "It rather soured me."

"Besides," the Queen Mother smiled, "you don't particularly like to go galloping out after that poor fox, do you?"

Diana smiled. "That doesn't make me against hunting."

"I suppose blood sports are all right," the Queen observed. "But they're not for me."

Prince Charles laughed. "I remember riding in a fox hunt when I was a school boy. You'd think I had personally murdered the fox! The National Society for the Abolition of Cruel Sports mounted an attack against me that made all the front pages. I put a stop to fox hunting right after that."

"As I recall," Prince Philip mused, "it was I who suggested you take up rugby."

"It wasn't until Anne began riding again a few years ago that I took up hunting again. But with a very low profile."

"That's quite a sensible arrangement," Nicholas Soames

said. "I mean, to take up cross-country racing, as they call it. It's just like hunting except that there isn't any fox."

"They call it steeplechase racing in America," said Prince Edward.

Charles turned to him. "I didn't know we had a Yankeephile in the family."

Prince Edward ignored the jibe. "How is Allibar working out?"

"Charles has purchased the most marvelous Irish chaser," the Queen Mother told Diana, if she hadn't followed the conversation. "A gelding. I think he's a marvelous mount!"

"Beautiful horse," Charles said enthusiastically. "I'm going to race him in the Grand National at Liverpool. But first, of course, the Grand Military Gold Cup at Sandown Park."

"*If* you qualify," Prince Philip said with a mordant smile. Diana sensed that there was some underlying disagreement between father and son.

"I have only three more races to run to qualify. I'll make it."

Prince Edward glanced at Diana. "It's a question of competition. When you're riding against the best, you may look the fool."

Charles did not agree. "My trainer says it's safer to compete against top amateurs rather than against unpredictable and dangerous riders."

"We shall see," said Prince Philip.

"I have to make fifteen rides in public before I can ride the Grand National," Charles told Diana. "I'll make it."

Parker-Bowles glanced at Diana. "Perhaps it's a bit much to talk horses when it's obvious the lady doesn't much like them."

"I love horses!" Diana protested. "It's just that I don't ride much."

"If at all," Parker-Bowles smiled.

"We don't do much riding up here at Balmoral," Charles said. The conversation seemed to lapse, and then suddenly broke up into separate groups. Diana ate in silence.

"But we do fish," Charles said, leaning toward her over the table, catching her eye.

"In the River Dee that flows by the castle?"

"Yes." Charles was suddenly animated. "It's one of the best salmon runs in the country. Maybe in the world. Do you fish?"

"For mackerel," said Diana, squirming a bit. She had nothing against fishing, but she simply had not become an active addict. "And I pot lobster."

Charles chuckled. "One thing about fishing. You don't have to compete with anyone. Only with the fish. In fact, it's pretty much a spectator sport, even if you're fly-casting yourself."

"It sounds delightful."

Charles was eyeing her carefully. She sensed that whatever he was going to say would be crucial.

"I'm going in the morning," he said. "Would you like to come along?"

"I'd love to!"

"You can watch. The best time to start is at the crack of dawn. Are you game?"

"Oh, yes!"

It was very close to dawn when Diana was aroused. She dressed quickly in her green Wellingtons, pants, sweater, head scarf, and a square-billed cap to protect her hair and head against the chilly, overcast weather. Charles appeared by her side in his waders, green jacket, vest gear, and cap.

In a moment they were outside the castle in the cold morning air, climbing into the green Range Rover that Diana remembered riding in not only with last night's detective, but with her brother-in-law as well.

Charles's golden Labrador retriever came yelping out of its kennel to join them in the car.

"Meet Harvey."

Diana made friends with the bouncy eager dog as Charles packed his rod in a rack attached to the side of the car. Then he climbed in.

"Ready?"

"All ready."

Something occurred to Charles. "Diana, we may not be alone out there."

Charles pointed down toward the river. "This is all Balmoral property on this side of the river. But the other side isn't."

Diana understood. "You mean there may be photographers."

"That's what I mean." He studied her with interest. "I didn't think you'd be prepared for that."

"I read the newspapers. I see the photos."

Charles started up the Range Rover. "I don't want them to snap us." His face was hard.

"Neither do I," Diana said. "But don't worry about me. I can take care of myself. You go right on and fish. I'll watch."

They drove down a little way from the castle and Charles pulled over to the side. Harvey leaped out of the car and plunged down the grassy slope toward the water. Charles got the rod from the rack. Diana followed him as he went down the slope to the water. She kept herself in the shelter of the trees. She had a very good view of the clear fresh water as it rolled over the rounded pebbles in the river bed.

Charles turned to her. "I'm going in!" He walked out into the swift current where the water seemed to boil up around him. He began a few tentative casts, but caught nothing.

Diana watched him closely. She could see that something seemed to be bothering him. He was concentrating not on the water but on the riverbank opposite them. Diana looked across. There seemed to be no one there at all.

She sat down in the grass and tightened the cap on her head. It was bitterly cold. Charles began moving against the current, but he had no luck. Oddly enough, Diana had the curious sensation of being watched. She glanced over her shoulder. There was Balmoral Castle rising in all its glory against the overcast sky; no one was in sight. She glanced across the River Dee. In the wooded area she thought she saw sudden movement.

When she looked again, she could make out nothing.

"Charles."

But he paid no attention. He was standing motionless in the water, looking at the bank, too. Diana turned around so that no one across the way could get a glimpse of her face. In a moment Charles came storming up the bank.

"Come on! Let's move. I know a better spot. It's less crowded!"

He grabbed her by the arm and the two of them ran up the slope to the car, Harvey barking and circling about them in great excitement.

Once in the Range Rover, Charles started it up, driving down the roadway along the riverbank into a much more secluded section of the woods.

"Paparazzi, or I miss my guess," he said briefly.

"Photographers?"

"Fleet Street's finest. They're always there. I don't want them bothering us." He looked at her. "I don't want them taking pictures of us together."

"Ashamed of me?" Diana asked with a quirky smile.

He snorted. "Not at all! But I'd like to enjoy a little privacy. Wouldn't you?"

Indeed, she would.

He bounced along almost six miles from the castle, and then pulled over and got out again. A brief reconnoiter established the fact that there was no one opposite them. The woods were more pronounced here, the pine trees giving shelter, and the oaks with their big leaves, providing a good screen against prying eyes and peeping cameras.

"Can't you buy the whole river and fence it in?" Diana asked with a laugh.

Charles made a face. "That wouldn't be playing the game, you know. Queen Caroline, she was Queen in 1727, George II's wife, once asked her favorite Prime Minister, Robert Walpole, how much it would cost to fence in Kensington Gardens, Hyde Park, Green Park, and St. James's Park for exclusive use by the royal family."

Charles mimicked Walpole: "Your Majesty, it would cost three crowns." Pause. "England, Ireland, and Scotland."

Diana giggled.

"You've got to remember that a crown was a coin not too long ago, before we got into this dreadful pence-pound thing. Worth five shillings."

"I'm not that young!" Diana protested. "I rmember what a crown is."

Charles shrugged and took up his pole. Harvey barked and frolicked about. In another moment, Charles was thigh-deep in the water and Diana had seated herself on a bank more or less hidden behind a tree. Watching Charles, she realized that he was more intent on surveying the grounds beyond the river than on the fish he was supposedly trying to catch. For a moment it almost seemed to her that he was using his rod to try to beat the salmon out of the water rather than to fly-fish in the traditional manner.

Then, quite suddenly, Diana did see someone in the trees on the other side of the River Dee. She moved behind the trunk of the tree where she was sitting and stood up. There was only one way to handle a photographer or reporter who might be nosing into things. She determined that they would not get her picture that morning. At the same time she was interested in them. Who were they? How had they found out that she was at Balmoral? Or did they even know who she was?

She took a hand mirror out of her bag and turned her back to the river. Holding the mirror up to her right eye, she stood behind the tree and moved the mirror around until she could see some movement halfway up the opposite bank. Sure enough, there was a man there—no, two. She watched carefully. Three.

They were looking at Prince Charles. One of them had a pair of binoculars. The man with the glasses was looking right into Diana's mirror. The sun had come out from behind the overcast sky and Diana flicked the mirror to throw the sun in the man's face. She saw another one holding a camera. He was very clear in the mirror. She laughed. He wasn't going to get a picture of her face!

Meanwhile Charles had spotted them but pretended he had not. Almost immediately Diana saw quick movement in the brush. Now only one man stood where there had been three. She turned the mirror and saw that one was heading downstream and the other upstream. She sensed that they were spreading out in order to cover her from two different angles; then, when she came out from behind the shelter of the tree, one of them would be able to take her picture.

Charles immediately assessed the strategy. He came running out of the water and waved to her. "Get back to the car!" he shouted.

She pulled her flat cap down tightly over her ears and adjusted the scarf so that little of her face showed. Then she ran up the bank to the car, keeping her face forward. Har-

vey followed her, yelping happily. Charles pulled a pair of
binoculars out of his gear. He put them up to his eyes.
They were larger than the ones the reporter held. Charles
focused the glasses and watched the man in the trees.

"I thought so," he grunted. Quickly he scrambled up the
bank and fastened his fishing rod to the rack. In a moment
he had climbed in and started the car.

Diana burst out into giggles. "It's just like a spy movie!"

He turned to gaze at her, and then quite suddenly his
face, stern and pale up to that moment, relaxed and he
threw back his head and roared.

"You did rather well, you know," he complimented her.
"I don't know where you got that mirror trick."

"Ladies always know what to do with mirrors," she said
pointedly.

He was studying her as he tooled the green Range Rover
along the road back to the castle. "You seem to take all this
in stride."

"I don't like people prying at me, and I know how to keep
them from doing it—if that's what you mean."

"You seem to thrive on this kind of adversity."

Diana shook her head. "I don't at all like it."

"But you stopped them from getting their picture."

"Who are they? Do you know?"

Charles turned to her, a smile curling his lips. "Oh, indeed I do. One was James Whitaker, of the *Daily Star*. He
was the one with the glasses. Another was Ken Lennox,
one of the London paparazzi. And the third was Arthur
Edwards, of the *Sun*."

"You know them that well?"

"Certainly. We're old—well, adversaries is a strong
word. But *friends* is a bit of a misstatement."

Diana smiled. "I'd love to see that picture they took of
me—or rather of my cap."

"I'm sure you will see it. We'll have to keep you home

this afternoon under cover when I go to the Highland
Games at Braemar." He grinned. "You're really all right,
do you know that?"

Diana was thinking of something else. "Will anyone tell
them who I am? I mean, they'll want to know, won't they?"

Charles considered. "They're probably playing games
right now trying to identify you." That gave him a further
thought. "It's going to be rough going back to London Sunday. They'll follow you. I'll have Nick and Andrew take
you through."

Diana translated that to mean that Nicholas Soames and
Andrew Parker-Bowles would be flying back to London
with her on the jet.

She and Charles spent the rest of the morning walking
through the more private sections of the woods on the other
side of the castle grounds, completely isolated from any
possible eavesdropping. They talked of all sorts of things—
many of them related to their early years together when
they really didn't know one another. They even discussed
the time they had spent together on the shoot at Althorp
when Charles was dating Lady Sarah.

When it came time for Charles to visit the Highland
Games, Diana stayed at the castle with the Queen Mother.
Charles put on his ceremonial tartan kilt and tweed jacket
and set out with the Queen and Prince Philip.

On his return that evening he was chuckling with amusement.

"They're climbing the walls, you know, trying to find
out who you are," he told Diana. "You're that 'mystery
woman,' if you can believe it. Oh, they'll probably find out.
They've got contacts everywhere, even inside the castle.
But they'll have a hard time anyway."

It was a delightful evening for Diana. She was sharing
something very special with Prince Charles. And appar-

ently Prince Charles was sharing something very special with her. Diana decided that no matter what happened in the future, no one could ever take away those wonderful hours she spent with him.

8

Prince Charles was true to his promise. When Lady Diana returned to Dyce Airport to board the plane for Heathrow she was accompanied by Nicholas Soames and Andrew Parker-Bowles. The two men helped her with her things and stood by waiting to board the plane with her.

A stranger approached.

"Reporters," Soames said in a low voice to Diana.

She studied the newcomer carefully. She had seen him before, in the wrong end of her pocket mirror. It was the man with the binoculars who had been spying on her Saturday morning.

At first the journalist pointedly ignored Diana, speaking briefly to Soames and Parker-Bowles, asking them routine questions about the weekend party at the castle. Quite smoothly he turned to Diana.

"Lady Diana Spencer?" he said softly. "I'm James Whitaker of the *Star*. Did you have a nice weekend?"

Diana felt embarrassed. She looked down, furious at herself for suddenly blushing. "Yes. Thank you very much."

"Hadn't we better be going?" Soames said to Diana, taking her arm and moving her away from the reporter.

"So they've found out who you are," Parker-Bowles observed as they found their seats on the plane

"Charles thought they might."

"They have people everywhere," said Soames.

Diana saw the journalist take a seat on the plane some rows in back of her. He was joined by several other men; she assumed they were journalists too. When the plane landed at Heathrow, her escorts took charge once again, herded her into a cab, and bundled her off to Coleherne Court. Soames kept looking back through the rear window of the cab to see if they were being followed.

"It's like a Sherlock Holmes picture," Diana giggled.

Soames glanced at her warily. "This is only the beginning, Diana."

She arrived at Block H Coleherne Court without incident, and within minutes was regaling her roommates with details of the weekend at Balmoral Castle. Just before midnight the telephone rang. It was Prince Charles.

"I wanted to make sure you had arrived safely. Was there any trouble at the airport?"

"You mean with the reporters?"

"Yes."

"There were several of them there. But Nick and Andrew took care of them properly. The *did* know my name."

"I thought as much." Charles sounded grim. "That means they'll have it in the morning papers. Well, we'll have to do something about that." He did not explore that line of thought, but switched immediately to another subject, his voice clearing up. "Let's talk about another fishing date. Would you like to come up again toward the end of the month?"

And the rest of the conversation involved a second trip to Balmoral.

The newspaper report next morning was brief, mentioning Lady Diana Spencer's name among the guests at Balmoral Castle. One of her co-workers at the kindergarten showed her the paper next morning; she found herself unable to resist blushing once again. In spite of the story, her working day was quite a normal one, and she spent the usual time working with her fifty children.

She was tired after her day's work and stayed home that night. It was after dinner that the telephone rang for her.

"They've been after you," her younger brother Charles told her.

"Who?"

"The reporters. They called this morning at the house. I answered the telephone. The man never said who he was, but I knew."

"What did you say?"

Charles was bubbling over now. "I told them that you were going to be with your boy friend tonight! At Wimbledon."

"Wimbledon?"

"On Viewfield Road."

"Very fashionable," Diana said, wondering what was coming next.

"And that's where they're going to hunt for you."

Diana frowned. "What are you up to, anyway?"

"Don't you see? It's one of my schoolmates at Eton! He lives there. It's a joke, Diana!"

To Diana it really didn't seem very funny. "You mean you told the reporter that I was dating one of your teeny-bopper friends?" Diana gasped. Then, abruptly, she saw the ligher side of it. She burst our laughing. "You didn't!"

"But I did!" he said, his voice gaining confidence. He had been afraid she would be angry. "I can't wait to hear what happened!"

Diana hung up thoughtfully. In the event they did fall for her brother's scurvy little trick—which was pretty funny, at that—she knew they would continue looking. It wouldn't take long to locate her after all. A few more telephone calls, a question here and there, and they'd be right on her doorstep. She knew that the group of them who had been in Scotland knew her by sight now. It would be impossible to dodge them forever.

She huddled with her roommates. "I'm afraid we're going to be under siege," she told them. "I don't know what to do but simply put up with it. But I'm warning you that there may be a lot of knocks on the door and if they get the phone number, a lot of telephone calls."

The very next morning Diana thought she was being followed when she went out shopping for milk and bread at a nearby Indian delicatessen. When she returned to the apartment she saw a car in which two men were watching the front of the building.

Diana showed her roommates the car she suspected; they kept a watch on it all the next day.

The morning of the third day the two watchers were waiting outside again. But this time, one of the journalists came forward and introduced himself to Carolyn Pride and asked when Diana would be coming out.

"In a few minutes."

Carolyn went back inside and told Diana what had happened. "He was very polite," she told Diana. "Said he didn't want to scare us by keeping watch that way. Wanted to know when you were coming out. It seems they'd like pictures."

Diana took a deep breath and let herself out of the apartment. Almost immediately two men came foward. One of them was the reporter she had met on Sunday at Dyce Airport.

"Could we take pictures?" he asked politely.

"Why, Mr. Whitaker?"

"Because you're very pretty. And because you're the girl who is bringing happiness back to Prince Charles."

"That's such a charming way of putting it!" she noted mockingly.

He shrugged.

"Well, all right," she said. "But don't be long. I have to go."

The photographer, whom Diana later learned was Frank Barrett, began taking shots of her. Whitaker got out his pad. "Is it true that you are in love with Prince Charles?" he asked.

Diana didn't know what to say. She didn't want to deny it; that would sound too easy and make it seem that she protested too much. She didn't want to confirm it. She said nothing. The two journalists followed her to her blue Volkswagen. She got in and drove away, waving at them.

On Friday the story appeared—the second one about Lady Diana Spencer. Charles was on the telephone to her later. "It's only the beginning," he warned her. "You'll have to get used to it."

The weekend went by without incident. Diana began to relax. Perhaps Charles was wrong. Perhaps everything would settle back to normal once the press became aware that there was no big romance on the wing.

Or was there?

By Thursday of the second week after her weekend at Balmoral, Diana had almost descended to earth again after her stratospheric flights of fancy with Charles. She was going to meet him later in the month in Scotland, but so far no actual plans had been made.

Meanwhile, Fleet Street had finally discovered that

Diana Spencer worked at Pimlico at the Young England Kindergarten. Telephone calls were fast and furious, interrupting the children's schedule.

Finally Kay Seth-Smith called her in to try to devise some system of appeasing the cameramen before the whole school routine became totally disrupted. What they decided on was a photographic session.

"That should satisfy them," Diana said. "I suppose they do have to make their living somehow."

"Maybe they'll just go home after it's done."

Diana knew that without a session, she would be under great pressure back at Coleherne Court until something broke.

And so the photo opportunity was set up for Thursday, September 17. Invitations were sent to Fleet Street.

It was a hot, very steamy day, typical of the muggy fall weather that descended on London regularly to make life miserable for everyone. Diana knew that it would be difficult to look cool and fresh; she selected a cotton gingham skirt she had bought at the Liberty store. It usually kept its press and looked especially appealing. It was one of her favorites.

When she got to school that morning Kay handed her a copy of the *Daily Mail*, opened to Nigel Dempster's "Diary." Dempster was the nearest thing in England to a national arbiter of the royal family's affairs. Diana started reading without quite realizing the impact of his story.

"Has Charles found his future bride?" Dempster asked rhetorically. The answer, according to the copy, was that Charles had, indeed. The new romance, Dempster pointed out, was in the very early stages. Anything could happen, of course, to spoil it or to help it. Dempster, however, was optimistic; he thought it would work out.

The lady was Diana Spencer. Accompanying the article

was a picture of the possible bride, unrecognizable in the view taken of her with her eyes cast down. The photos taken by Whitaker's photographer associate had not yet appeared; they wanted a picture of Charles *and* Diana.

The crux of the story was Dempster's report that in the circle of Prince Charles's friends—especially within the tight, charmed little sphere of his female confidantes, Lady Tryon and Camilla Parker-Bowles—Diana Spencer was definitely reported to be the front runner. According to Dempster, they had "both given the heir to the throne their approval over his new choice of a girl friend."

And: "Now the way is clear for Charles to plight his troth to Lady Diana Spencer, who, friends tell me, has secretly worshipped him for most of her life."

Diana was appalled. Where had this journalist received his information? How had he known? Certainly she knew Kanga—Lady Tryon—and Camilla Parker-Bowles. Had Charles advised them to talk? Were they doing it on their own? Who was behind this?

The first of the cameramen were already outside, waiting in front of the school for Diana Spencer to appear for the picture session. Diana immediately selected two of her small charges, and appeared at the front door of the school building, a brick structure formerly a Boy Scout hut.

The crowd of journalists and photographers surged forward. Diana told them clearly that she didn't want to give the names of the two girls because their parents had not been consulted. The photographers agreed.

"And I please don't want to answer too many questions. Agreed?"

Not necessarily. There were murmurs, but that was all.

It was morning and the sun was rising at a steep angle. Diana sat on the ground with a child on each side of her, looking cool and sedate, even in the heat. There were cherry trees in the background of the school garden, and it was all very English-garden enchantment and old-fashioned landscape serene.

The sun began casting a shadow over the garden from a church located in St. George's Square, on which the school faced. Although they tried to shade their lenses with sun-screens, the picture-takers were getting bad light.

"Lady Diana," one of the paparazzi said, "could you please move out of the dark and let the sun light up your skin and hair?"

Diana complied. Although she was not a professional photographer, both her sisters had worked on *Vogue* and knew something about pictures. What they were looking for was the halo effect, with the sun at the side, making her hair into a blaze of light around her face.

She picked up one of the children and took the other by the hand, walking across the playground, out into the light with the sun coming from behind her. The photographers began snapping pictures even before she stopped to pose. It was odd, but for a long moment there was not a sound from the usually loudly talking and laughing group. Diana was puzzled.

"About Prince Charles," said one of the reporters after a long interval of picture taking.

"I don't want to say anything about him, please," Diana said softly.

"How do you feel about him?" another asked.

"You know I can't say anything about him."

"Have you been instructed by Buckingham Palace not to talk?" Whitaker asked.

"No. That isn't true. I decided not to myself."

By now there were more groups of photographers arriv-ing. Linked to the Nigel Dempster article that morning, the photographic session would provide great news leads for all papers. Even though it was getting hot in the garden and she was a bit tired of smiling and trying to keep her poise, she continued to let them take their pictures.

She broke for lunch with her two charges. As she was eating, a representative of the Press Association, a news picture agency, arrived at the Kindergarten to ask if they too could join the session. The man asking Diana had a copy of the *Evening Standard* in his hand with one of the early-morning photographs printed on the front page.

"Yes," Diana agreed, and took the newspaper from him to see how the pictures had come out. One glance was enough. Diana Spencer was all over the front page. But that wasn't the nasty part of the surprise. The nasty part was the fact that because of the heat of the day she had not worn a slip under her skirt. The Liberty print had betrayed her; it was almost totally a see-through fabric, especially back-lighted by the powerful morning sun. The bright light shining through from behind revealed her legs and her chic briefs clearly enough for all the world to see.

She wanted to die. She clutched the newspaper in her hand and retired to the school's rest room. She was weeping softly, trying to keep herself poised. After a few bad minutes she returned to the pressmen who were waiting, her face again in total control.

"What can I do to get this picture out of the paper?"

"Nothing," the Association man said. "By tomorrow morning you'll find yourself in a whole lot of other newspapers."

The pictures they took that afternoon were not back-lighted. But the pictures that hit the papers that afternoon and the next morning were all backlighted and all of them were on page one. Diana was beside herself with chagrin all afternoon, even though she tried to pose for the photographers with assurance. When she left for the day, she was weary and terribly depressed.

She wanted to sink into the floor. Her roommates all

sympathized. But they were almost alone. The world—not just England—saw her the next morning in all her glory. DI IS BLUSHING, one headline read coyly. Another put it: LADY DIANA'S SLIP. Or lack of slip.

Diana worried constantly about the reaction of Prince Charles. When he telephoned that night, she steeled herself against a tirade from him, mostly about her stupidity and naiveté. But after a few words of greeting, he mentioned that he had seen the photographs.

"I knew your legs were good, but I didn't realize they were that spectacular."

Diana closed her eyes. There were tears of sudden relief in them. He wasn't all that angry. She knew that he could have taken a sudden dislike to the situation—and she could have been the cause of it all.

"Did you really have to show them to everybody?" he asked her, chuckling a bit.

After some more conversation, Charles became serious.

"We've got to handle this thing differently. You were tricked into this. I'm not going to let you be tricked again."

"I wasn't tricked," Diana insisted. "It was my own fault."

"Whatever. We've got to play this thing in a very low-key way. There's no sense having pictures of us in every edition."

"How can we do that?"

"We'll just keep out of sight."

"They know me now."

"That's why we'll be meeting next in Allington. At the home of the Parker-Bowleses."

"But that's ninety miles from London!"

Charles laughed. "They can't say you don't know your geography!"

He set the date for a weekend in early October and told her how to get there.

9

Diana Spencer found the Wiltshire home of the Parker-Bowleses without trouble on Friday night and discovered that she had arrived before Prince Charles. Although she had met Camilla several times before, she did not know her well. They began talking in the sparring, tentative way of people who knew about each other but weren't well acquainted, until finally both began to relax and enjoy one another's company.

By the time Parker-Bowles and Prince Charles arrived, Diana and Camilla were on the best of terms and were laughing and joking about people they knew and things they had heard about them. One of their earlier exchanges had concerned Charles.

"He's riding tomorrow at West Midlands, you know," Camilla had said.

"Charles?" Diana hadn't heard about that.

"Yes." Camilla watched Diana intently. "He didn't tell you, did he?"

"Not at all. It was simply a weekend in which to dodge the press."

Camilla was amused. "It's his sporting blood," she said dryly. "We're to go to watch. The press won't be able to tie us up with him, but they'll know you're watching him."

"He's taunting them, then."

"We'll be going to Lambourn first thing. That's where we're picking up Judy."

"Who's Judy?"

"Judy Gaselee. Nick Gaselee's wife." Camilla frowned. "Heavens! You haven't been briefed, have you?"

Diana looked dazed.

"Nick Gaselee is Charles's horse trainer; he's in charge of Allibar. Charles is very much into cross-country racing. That's what this is all about."

"But isn't West Midlands at Ludlow, in Shropshire?"

"Yes. We're going to be up very early tomorrow, my dear."

"It sounds exciting," Diana said vaguely.

"There's more. A surprise. Charles wants you to see Highgrove."

Diana showed her complete ignorance.

"He's house-hunting. You're to approve or disapprove." She studied Diana. "He wants your approval."

Parker-Bowles and Prince Charles arrived together and after dinner they sat around the blazing fire chatting about everything and nothing. Gradually Charles outlined the weekend ahead, and it conformed exactly with Camilla's prediction. Because of the action-filled morning planned, Charles suggested an early bedtime and they were all quite soon sleeping.

Rising early, they stood around drinking coffee and warming up. It was October and the countryside was chilly. Diana had dressed in her boots, pants, and sweater to keep warm, and then threw on her sporty green coat over that.

They left and drove quickly over to Lambourn, Diana and Charles in his blue estate car, and Camilla and Parker-Bowles in their own car. Charles's detectives were following at a discreet distance in a souped-up Land Rover.

At Lambourn, Diana met Nick Gaselee and his wife Judy. Judy joined Diana and Camilla in the Parker-Bowles car, with Charles and his trainer driving over to pick up Allibar from the stables for the drive to Ludlow. There wasn't much to talk about on the drive, and Diana found herself dozing as the car made its way through Gloucestershire and Worcestershire to Shropshire.

Her spirits picked up a bit when they finally reached West Midlands and got into the box reserved for them. Parker-Bowles had left the party for London. Camilla and Judy and Diana were alone in the box. But not quite all that much alone.

Diana noticed a familiar face in the crowd of people milling about in front of the box. It was the reporter she had spotted in September.

"Good morning, Mr. Whitaker," she said, deciding to go on the offensive immediately.

Whitaker nodded and smiled. "Mrs. Parker-Bowles. Mrs. Gaselee." He knew them all. But he wanted to talk to Diana. "Are you betting on Prince Charles today?"

"Ah. Is Prince Charles racing?" Diana looked him in the eye.

"He's racing Allibar."

Diana studied her program. "Yes. I'm betting on Allibar—to place."

"Does he know you're here?" Whitaker asked.

"Allibar?"

"Prince Charles."

"Possibly," she responded airily.

Whitaker retired with a smile. Shortly after that Prince Charles appeared on Allibar. Diana could feel the excitement of the imminent race; she began to wave her arms and shout. So did Camilla and Judy, although neither of them were a bit demonstrative.

With a surge the horses were off. The crowd gave a roar. The jockeys were pushing their mounts over the fences around the three-mile course.

By the time Charles had made the final fence, Diana was standing up and jumping in her excitement. Charles moved up into second place. Could he win? Diana was too excited to watch carefully, but she screamed encouragement and cheered him on loudly.

He came in number two—exactly as she had bet on him.

Diana and her companions rushed out of the box and down to the unsaddling enclosure to welcome him in after the race. Even down there, protected from the photographers and the press, Diana made sure that the two of them were never close enough together to afford anyone an opportunity to get them in one frame of a picture.

Fleet Street had come alive. Diana was appalled at the pandemonium that had broken out all over the track. The word was obviously out. Dozens of reporters and photographers were arriving from London to get pictures of her and Charles. The first there, like Whitaker and several others, had obviously telephoned for reinforcements. They were swarming all over the race course. And Diana knew that she was the object of their search.

"Take care of her!" Charles told Camilla as he turned to face the reporters and get out of his racing gear. Quickly Camilla and Judy took Diana in hand, guiding her down to the nearest women's restroom. There she hid as Camilla and Judy went out to reconnoiter and bring back reports on the situation outside.

It was a long time before the reporters and photographers began to thin out. But eventually the way was cleared and Diana came out with Camilla and Judy. They drove back to Lambourn, dropped Judy off, and then went on to Wilt-shire. Shortly after they arrived, Prince Charles came in with his detectives in tow.

Diana needed a rest. She awoke refreshed in time for dinner. Afterward, they talked about the press. Charles was annoyed at them for their persistence, but he under-stood why they were the way they were.

"They haven't seen you for a month. They're interested in you."

"Interested!" Camilla repeated. "They almost tore apart the track!"

"We're going to have to keep a lower profile," Charles mused. "I think I know what we'll have to do."

Diana waited for him to explain. He did not, instead turning to another consideration. "Tomorrow we're going up to Gloucestershire."

"Ah," said Camilla, looking at Diana.

"To see Highgrove."

And that was exactly what they did. Highgrove was located just off A433 after Doughton, a marketing town near Tetbury, in Gloucestershire. Charles drove off A433 into a half-mile-long gravel drive leading up to the front of the three-story manor house built over two hundred years before.

Set in among the greenery of the surrounding woods, Highgrove had an old-fashioned Georgian look to it, al-though it was not a typically Georgian house. Diana and Charles got out of the car in front of the imposing white double doors that led into the entryway. Diana looked up at the bulky front with its enormous nine- and twelve-paned windows set into the clay-yellow facade.

"It was built originally for a man with a funny name—

John Paul Paul. About 1796 or 1798 I think the real estate agent said."

Refurbished several times since, it was at the time owned by Maurice Macmillan, the son of England's former prime minister, and a publisher and politician in his own right.

Charles opened the door with the key. Diana looked up into the enormous entrance hall, more than forty feet in length, with a broad staircase sweeping up to the second floor. To the left there was an enormous reception room; to the right there was another one.

They went into one of the reception rooms, staring about at the now empty areas, imagining what could be put into them to bring them to life. Nearby they found the drawing room, with its center of interest an imposing marble fireplace rising from a magnificent polished-oak floor. The mantelpiece, of Irish marble, was decorated with a carved dolphin, the heraldic emblem of Tetbury nearby.

"How do you like it?" Charles asked.

The truth of the matter was that it was not nearly as imposing a place as Althorp, Diana thought, but it had a charm of its own.

"It's lovely," she said.

Diana looked behind Charles through a bay window out onto a formal garden in back of the house. Beside the bay window stood a pair of French doors. Diana gazed through them, following the long walkway lined by sculptured golden yews and ending up in an old-fashioned pool covered with lily pads. She could see an enormous cedar of Lebanon in the center of the garden.

Beyond the drawing room was the library with bookshelves fitted into two walls. They wandered through the butler's pantry, the kitchen with its stone-flagged floor and old-fashioned solid-fuel stove, and into the billiard room, and then back to the dining room.

From outside, Diana had noticed that there was one large

wing attached to the main part of the house. This was the nursery. The entire wing was devoted to it, in fact, with a 19-foot by 15-foot nursery room with an open fireplace and a toy cupboard. Included in the wing were bedrooms for a nanny and her maid and two separate rooms joined by a bath.

They went out through the French doors and into the garden. Charles led Diana through a pathway to the side of the mansion. There stood the stables, with powder-blue sectioned doors and stone masonry walls. The heads of horses looked out at them.

"Ah, then," Diana said teasingly, "*this* is what it's all about!"

"Aren't they nice?" Charles sauntered over, gentling a brown mare and turning to Diana. "It's a nice locality. Anne lives at Gatcombe Park." Diana knew that Captain Mark Phillips, Charles's brother-in-law, a retired army officer, now worked as a gentleman farmer and show jumper only several miles from Highgrove.

"It's the hunting you really like here, isn't it, Charles?" Diana asked softly.

Charles nodded. "Yes. It's Beaufort Hunt country."

While Diana did not really *like* to hunt, she knew all about hunting. England was divided up into about two hundred different areas, each marked out for a specific hunt. In Gloucestershire, the hunt was controlled by the Dukes of Beaufort; the hunt itself was called the Beaufort. It had always been the most popular hunt with the royal family.

The Beaufort Hunt extended over 760 square miles of the choicest countryside in England. Highgrove was square in the middle of Beaufort. Princess Anne had settled down at Gatcombe Park because of the hunt; now that Charles had begun to take up fox hunting once again, he had decided to do it in the best area.

"There are 346 acres of prime farmland attached," Charles said as the two of them gazed about at the rolling Cotswold countryside.

"I can fancy you as a gentleman farmer," Diana giggled.

They continued poking about the estate, walking under the trees and strolling on the grass. They exchanged quips and bits and pieces of conversation. Diana experienced a slight pang of disappointment. She did not really feel that Charles was all that attentive to her, even in the lovely intimacy of the manor house and estate.

He seemed preoccupied. Was he still mooning over Anna Wallace? The thought of her sent a chill into Diana's heart. Perhaps he was simply seeing Diana, dating her, using her like some kind of new plaything that would soon wear out like new fads always do. Or perhaps he fancied her as a pleasant, affable new horse for his stable.

"Do you like it?" he asked her again, almost in a pleading tone.

"I like it," Diana told him.

He nodded, much the way a businessman might nod when he had made a particular decision.

Although they held hands as they walked and although he kissed her briefly as they stood by the pond with its lily pads, the sense of intimacy that had held them together at Balmoral was gone. Diana did not know if it would ever come back. What had happened? she wondered. Where was his mind now?

It was most certainly not on her.

On this downbeat note the weekend came to a conclusion, with Diana driving home alone in her blue Volkswagen. Prince Charles had numerous affairs of state to attend to after his weekend at the Parker-Bowleses. Diana rested, straightening up things at the apartment, picking up her laundry, and doing the usual shopping chores to keep the apartment well stocked.

"The photographers found you at Ludlow, didn't they?" Carolyn asked her one evening.

"There was almost a riot, Carolyn!"

"That's only the first time they've found you with him after Balmoral," Anne observed.

"They're out after blood," Diana sighed. "Charles says he has a way to fix them."

He telephoned that same night. After the usual round of greetings, he lowered his voice. It was suddenly almost as if the two of them were in a conspiracy of some kind.

"We'll have dinner tomorrow night. Do you know where the Windsor Castle Pub is?"

"I can find it." Diana almost asked him about the cuisine, but refrained. He was acting very odd.

"It's in Kensington Heights. Meet me in front of it tomorrow at seven."

Diana hung up, mystified.

Nevertheless, she was there at the specified time. Charles drew up to the curb and parked his car. He was driving a model she had never seen before. His Special Branch man sat in the passenger's seat.

"Come with me," Charles said, and got out of the car. He took her hand and started across the street with her. She looked up at the elegant modern apartment building facing the Windsor Castle Pub.

"Who lives here?"

Prince Charles simply smiled.

They went inside. The foyer was discreet, elegant, and very tastefully decorated. There was no one about. Charles rang for the elevator.

Since Charles would not talk, Diana remained silent.

They entered and rose to the top of the building, to the floor labeled "P" on the button. Diana was more and more puzzled. Who lived in a penthouse in this fabulous little hideaway? Still without a word, Charles led her out of the

elevator and to a door at the end of the corridor. It was the
only door on the floor. He took out a key chain, flicked one
key into the lock, opened the door, and let her in before
him.

He snapped on the lights as he joined her.

She found herself standing in a simply marvelous apartment, with wide windows overlooking Greater London,
bright now with night lights, and sparkling with its own
kind of magic. The apartment itself was magnificent. Diana
found herself staring in disbelief at a collection of gold objets d'art, porcelain, and silver, scattered around the room
casually but provocatively.

"What *is* this place?" Diana asked. "Whose are these?"

"Mine," Charles said. "Let me have your coat."

Mutely, she surrendered her coat. Now she saw the
paintings of seascapes and ships hung on the walls. She
went over to study them; they were originals, beautifully
mounted and framed.

Charles had disappeared with her coat. After a moment
he reappeared. She was running her hand along the damask
upholstering of an expensive cushioned chair.

"All right," Diana said. "It's obvious that this is your
apartment. There have been rumors around for years that
you had a hideaway right in the heart of London."

He shrugged. "As you can see, the rumors are true."

"You never hinted to me that there was such a place," she
said slowly.

"It only came evident last weekend that we needed somewhere to meet away from prying eyes."

The furnishings must have cost thousands, she thought,
studying them with an unpracticed eye.

He sat down on the comfortable divan and motioned her
to join him. With a reluctance she was at a loss to explain,
she did so.

"The furniture comes from one of the Queen's residences," he explained vaguely.

"It's beautiful."

He nodded. "Of course." He was acting strangely, calm, and cool, but at the same time, with a somewhat subdued stealth.

"Charles, why did you bring me here?" She felt herself flushing, her neck and shoulders hot.

"For dinner. Candlelight and wine." He smiled. "Are you hungry?"

"I'm starved. I thought we would be eating at the Windsor Castle Pub."

He frowned in honest bewilderment. "Whatever gave you that idea?"

She burst out laughing. "It was the obvious conclusion!"

"Oh, I see." He smiled. Then he rose and led her into the adjoining room. It was smaller than the main room, designed especially for dining. There was a polished walnut dining table that could seat from two to eight people. It was already set, with the food beautifully displayed in sterling serving dishes.

Charles lighted the wicks on the candles placed at each end of the table and lowered the lights. The wall switch was equipped with a rheostat that dimmed the electric bulbs in the chandelier above the table.

Through the window which Diana was facing she could see all the way to the Thames. The lights of London were spectacular.

"Oh, Charles," she said. The sight outside was so beautiful it almost brought tears to her eyes.

They started to eat.

"You'll be coming to Sandringham for my birthday party," Charles announced in the middle of the meal.

"Thank you."

He chuckled. "There's already word out that I'm going to announce my engagement on that occasion."

"Engagement? To whom?" Diana stared full into Charles's eyes. His were steady on hers.

"Of course it's all poppycock."

"Then you *aren't* going to announce your engagement."

"It's rather difficult when I simply am not engaged."

When they had finished the rather plain fare that Charles and the royal family preferred to eat, Diana rose and walked over to the window, looking out. She was standing there, her thoughts ascending in a kind of quiet and rhapsodic euphoria, when quite suddenly, she felt him next to her. Then his hands were around her waist and he was snuggling his head against her.

She took a quick breath, gave a start, and then deliberately relaxed. Charles was not too much a demonstrative type. They had been together, and alone, but usually in the woods or the wilds. He had kissed her before, of course, but those were simply parting kisses, almost brother and sister kisses. This was quite different.

Her pulse quickened. She could feel her heart pounding against her ribs. She knew he could feel her excitement, too. The thought of that unnerved her. She wanted to break away from him, but immediately forced herself not to move. She had wanted this intimacy for years—all her life. Now that she had it. . .

"Charles," she said softly, her eyes half closed.

"Yes?"

She turned toward him. His face was inches from hers. His eyes were watching her steadily. His arms entwined her back; he moved to meet her lips. There was a rushing sound, her own blood pounding through her head, and she was aware that she was being caressed and kissed thoroughly by a man who knew exactly how to kiss for maximum effectiveness.

She knew she must break loose before it was too late. Her own willpower was wilting. She wanted it to go on forever, but at the same time she didn't.

"Charles," she whispered desperately. He let her go and stood there, smiling at her with that crooked smile that was so familiar and so beloved.

"Yes, love?"

"Did you bring her here, too?" Diana's words choked in her throat.

"Did I bring whom here?" She was conscious of his deliberate English, his clipped tone, his anger.

"That woman. Anna Wallace."

His face went almost white. She could see the pulse beating hard in his neck. His eyes were angry blue, almost fiery. A sudden fear ran through her. Had she brought up the one wrong name at the wrong moment?

"I want to know." She was letting her own annoyance surface. "Is this your love nest?"

He moved toward her, his eyes flat. "It's anything you want to make of it, darling." He reached out and held her in his arms. When he tried to pull her toward him, she resisted. He looked down at her feet. She wondered why he was interested in them.

"I think, sir," she said softly, "you've made a bad mistake."

"I?" he responded. "Perhaps."

"I thought you knew me better than that," she told him, her voice hardening.

"Do you know yourself that well?" he asked in a cynical tone that jarred her.

"So this is where it all ends, isn't it?" She tried to steady her voice. "This is the end of all the hopes and all the dreams."

"It doesn't need to be."

"It does."

His face, hard and expressionless, lifted to hers. "Are you saying no to me?" His mouth twitched at the corner, that tic that sometimes appeared.

She thrust against his chest with her palms. Suddenly she realized how incredibly strong he was. She knew he was in excellent physical shape, but she had not been aware of the force of his masculinity. Now she wanted him to get away from her.

"Charles," she gasped.

He was holding her close now, kissing her throat.

She thrust her hands against him again and pushed away, breaking his grasp. She staggered slightly, off balance, and went down on the divan, sliding into it in an awkward pose.

"It's not the way I want it!" she said. Her face was hot and there were tears in her eyes. She wanted to scream at him.

He came over and stared down at her. His anger was consuming him now. She could see the venom in his eyes, the white of his cheeks, the trembling of his hands. The tic had returned, like something out of an old Humphrey Bogart movie.

Then he was gone. In a moment he stood there with her coat.

"Nor I," he said. "I see I've made a rather gigantic mis-calculation."

They descended in the elevator like two stone statues. Diana felt that there was no lower she could fall. Even when the elevator finally stopped, she was still going deeper and deeper into her own personal hell.

10

Somehow Diana Spencer was able to struggle through the next few days without letting anyone suspect her total frustration and hopelessness over her relationship with Prince Charles. She could not help displaying an uncharacteristic moodiness in front of her roommates, which they noticed immediately. However much they questioned her, she would not let any of her private thoughts and feelings find expression.

Within herself, she realized that she had stepped across a line—a line that was invisible but nevertheless definite. One simply did not say no to a man like Prince Charles. He *was* the heir apparent. He *would* be king. What right actually had she to refuse his affections?

Yet at the same time, Diana knew that she had acted completely in character. She was not a frivolous woman. She did not subscribe totally to the rather casual sexual mores of the time. She knew now that she did love Charles;

she loved him, really, enough to refuse him. The old-fashioned virtues meant something to her. If he had not learned that by now, quite probably he would never learn. Nor had he been paying attention to the various signals she had given him about her code of living.

In her frustration, Diane could quite easily rationalize it all in her mind. But when she recalled the stricken look on Charles's face, and when she remembered the anger he had displayed at her attitude, she would give anything she had to be back there at that moment and perhaps explain her feelings to him.

Later in the week Anne handed Diana the telephone. "It's for you."

It was Charles. He was normal, cool, and confident. "I haven't seen you," he said for starters.

She waited. What kind of reaction did he expect from that asinine remark?

"Princess Margaret is celebrating her birthday on November fourth," Charles went on.

"But I thought her birthday was in August."

"It is, this is a belated party," he explained. "I'd like you to come."

Diana knew that Charles's Aunt Margaret was one of his favorite people in the royal family. Certainly he would be there to celebrate with her. She felt relief that he had thought of her at all, given the situation between them.

"I'd love to," Diana said.

"There's going to be a big party at the Ritz Hotel."

He sounded completely impersonal. For that matter, so did she. If things were on, all right; if things were off, all right, too.

"How have you been?" he asked finally, in a tentative, searching manner.

"Fine." It all sounded so abrupt and stupid. She threw down all barriers and gave a half groan. "I've missed you!"

There was a brief silence. When he spoke again, his voice sounded odd. "Well, then, I'll see you Tuesday night at the Ritz!"

She hung up, noticing that her hands were warm and filmed with perspiration. Immediately she went to her room and shut the door. Was it on again? she wondered. Or was it really off permanently, with this the final scene?

There would be others in the family going to the party. She would go with someone else. At a royal family celebration, Charles would not be expected to come by to pick her up. She couldn't help noticing that he *had* sounded abrupt.

The Ritz Hotel on Piccadilly was crowded on Tuesday night, when Princess Margaret celebrated her fiftieth birthday. The paparazzi were out in force, but the hotel security staff kept them out of the huge ballroom. Plenty of flash bulbs popped as Diana scurried through the foyer on her way to the ballroom.

Finally she was inside. She found her place next to Prince Charles's and sat down. She could see him across the way, chatting with a group of palace staffers. She glanced across his empty place and got one of the most severe shocks of her life. Lady Jane Wellesley was seated on the other side of Charles. She murmured a subdued hello, as did Lady Jane from her side. They found themselves staring at one another across the empty seat with veiled curiosity.

During the dinner, which began soon afterward, Charles was his old ingratiating self. He had what might be considered a kind of overdrive gear in which he drove in public, especially on occasions of state. He adopted that mode of behavior. He divided his attention equally between Diana and Jane.

Diana noticed that Lady Jane seemed to be as surprised and chagrined as Diana to find that Charles was sharing his evening with two women. But she had been at the game longer than Diana and never let on at all. She had learned to cover up her feelings and pangs in the years of her attachment to Charles.

Prince Charles seemed quite amused about everything; although he was chatting with both Diana and Jane, he seemed to be more concerned about what was happening everywhere else in the room. Diana could hear the whispers; everyone was talking about the unexpected appearance of Diana and Jane together.

In a way, it was a nightmare. Charles was attentive to her, as attentive as usual, but at the same time, she felt that she was being *shared*.

Obviously, that was the way Charles wanted it. Was he tormenting her, putting her in her place, making her regret their last meeting? Was it all over? Was this simply the final scene? With Charles, it was difficult to tell exactly what he was feeling.

At the end of the evening, she returned to Coleherne Court. She fell into an exhausted sleep without tossing and turning and thinking about what had happened—or what had not happened.

A glance at the newspapers the next day surprised her considerably. While she had been thinking about how distant Charles acted, the public had been thinking how close he and Diana Spencer were! It seemed to be one of the supreme ironies of her relationship with Charles. As she felt her stock dropping, the observers felt her stock rising.

"Prince Charles could hardly keep his eyes off Diana, even though he was seated next to Jane Wellesley." Another speculation: "Is Prince Charles using Jane Wellesley as part of the old shell game he's been playing for years, using Lady Jane to take the heat off his *real* love, Diana Spencer?"

Diana didn't hear from Charles for several days. It was

becoming more and more amusing to leaf through the newspapers and read paragraphs about her and her love affair with the Prince of Wales. Amusing, in a masochistic kind of way.

Diana had forgotten one thing. November 14 was a significant date, more significant than simply Charles Windsor's thirty-second birthday. The Fleet Street pack knew that a birthday would be a perfect time to announce his engagement—especially with speculation so high about this brand-new heart interest of his.

Then on Sunday, November 9, Diana was astounded to read the *Sun*'s flat prediction that Prince Charles would announce his engagement to Diana Spencer during his birthday celebration at Sandringham on the upcoming Friday.

On Monday, the paparazzi were out in force once again at the Young England Kindergarten. The telephone rang continually at Coleherne Court. Journalists, friends, and total strangers were on the line, asking questions and making suggestions.

The week was a hectic one. So much interest had been stirred by the *Sun*'s prediction that Sir Larry Lamb, its editor, became the guru of the cause. Independent Television's *News at Ten* devoted a major part of one program entirely to Diana Spencer.

Nigel Dempster was interviewed. He stated flatly that the engagement would *not* be announced at the Prince of Wales's birthday party. Dempster offered to bet one thousand pounds with Sir Larry Lamb that nothing would happen on Friday.

The next day he doubled his bet, and on the third day, had four thousand pounds at stake.

"What will you do if you are proved wrong?" he was asked.

"I shall end it all," Dempster remarked serenely.

By that time Diana's outlook had improved considerably. She had talked with Charles again. He wanted her to be present at his birthday party at Sandringham. The party would take place at Wood Farm, one of the Queen's residences on the Sandringham estate, not far from the main house.

"So it's time for you to put Plan A into action," Charles joked.

Diana felt weak in the knees. Charles finally sounded his old self again. That meant that he had been playing games with her on Princess Margaret's birthday. At least there was hope for them.

"What's Plan A?"

For a moment Charles explained what he meant by the "plan," then he said, "I'll see you Friday," and hung up.

All week Coleherne Court was under siege. There were always a corps of reporters and paparazzi waiting outside to be sure Diana was there or not. A bunch was always watching the kindergarten, too.

On Friday morning Diana looked out the window and saw Number One Fleet Street Surveillance Group standing guard. Number Two was probably at the kindergarten; they would be frustrated because Diana was not going to work that day.

She called Carolyn, Virginia and Anne around her. "You all know what to do. Simply say that I'm not in if they ring up. And if they knock on the door, say I've gone out."

Carolyn giggled. "They'll simply go out of their minds when they find you've gone."

"Unless somebody's smart enough to trace your new car," Anne suggested.

Diana said, "They're not *that* smart. It's going to be delivered to my sister's place at Kensington Palace."

"Good luck," said Carolyn. She went over to the window, drew back the curtains and peered out. "They're still there, waiting."

Diana peered over her shoulder. She had been using the family's blue Renault during the week; without telling anyone, she had traded her Volkswagen for a new car. The Volks had been in several smashups and needed extensive repairs. Besides, Charles had made some comments about Diana's choice in cars—German, French, and everything but British.

Making sure the reporters were still watching the Renault, she said goodbye and slipped out the back way. What made it possible to use this subterfuge was the fact that she had never avoided the front entrance since Fleet Street had found her digs.

She hailed a cab on Earl's Court Road and directed the cabby to Kensington Palace. On the way she made sure no one was following her. At Kensington Palace she hurried over to the Barracks to see her sister Jane, kissed the baby, and then accompanied Jane out into the parking lot where her brand new red Mini Metro had been delivered the night before.

"Isn't it a lovely car?" her sister said.

Diana got in, started it up, and drove quickly out the gate after being checked through by the security guard. Within minutes she was on A10 heading north for Cambridge and eventually Sandringham. After a while she relaxed and let her hands take control of the car. She did not push it too hard; after all, it was brand new and needed breaking in gently.

Once in a while she would let out a little giggle of triumph, thinking of the journalists hanging around Coleherne Court watching her car and waiting for her to show up. She made the one-hundred-thirty mile trip without incident, pulling in through a side road to the Sandringham estate, which she knew intimately from past experience. She parked her car at the side of Sandringham House.

There were people outside the gates as usual when the Queen was in residence, but Diana did not think any of them had recognized her. Any journalist would have been looking for her blue Volkswagen or family Renault. Besides, as she learned when she got to Wood Farm, most of the Fleet Street gang were out with Prince Charles on his usual morning hunt.

Diana telephoned Coleherne Court. "Are they still waiting around for me?"

Carolyn laughed. "Yes. You've never seen a more dispirited bunch. We've all been in and out. They think you must be here. Or that you've disappeared completely."

"Perhaps they'll leave when they find I've gone."

"They've been taking pictures of the curtains, even."

Diana then telephoned her sister Lady Jane to tell her that she had arrived safely and without incident.

"Sarah telephoned," Jane told her. "She says one of those reporters visited her this morning. He wanted to know about your 'engagement.'"

What did Sarah tell him?"

"She asked them what they were going to do when Charles didn't announce your engagement this evening."

"Well, I wonder, too," Diana mused.

"One of the evening papers that just came in says you've vanished off the face of the earth."

Prince Charles came back from the hunt ravenously hungry and weary from the long day's riding. He greeted Diana with his usual reserved affection, and, still shivering from the chilling cold that permeated the countryside that day, went upstairs to clean up. When he returned to relax by the fire, he began chuckling over the successful execution of Plan A to confuse the press.

"The paparazzi are going crazy out there!" he told her with suppressed glee. "It's bitter cold. The wind off The Wash is full of frostbite. They're sitting in their cars trying to keep warm by smoking and idling the motors."

Diana felt a pang of solicitude. She remembered her sister's work in publications. "They're just doing their job."

"Oh, I know." Charles's eyes glinted. "But sometimes their job is to make me feel like a captive prince. I don't entirely like it."

"Happy birthday, Charles," Diana told him. She gave him his presents, which she had purchased at Harrods in Knightsbridge several days before. He began opening them as she watched with amusement.

"What can you buy for the man who has everything?"

"Two sensible plain white shirts," Charles announced, holding them up. "Collar size fifteen and a half."

"It does seem a bit silly," Diana confessed, "but I had a terrible time trying to figure out what to get you."

"Diana! I thank you very much. I suppose I should take these out for the paparazzi to photograph and write their clever captions. PRINCE OF WALES IN SHIRTY MOOD."

Diana giggled. "Let's forget about the paparazzi, Charles!"

"I find it rather difficult to forget them. Where did you park your car? They'll be catching on soon enough."

She told him.

"We'll have it locked up in one of the garages. Somebody may have seen you drive in. There are too many of them to expect complete privacy."

The Prince of Wales's thirty-second birthday party was a low-keyed affair, with most of the royal family and close relatives present. There were toasts and speeches, and joshing and laughter—the kind of very in-house jokes that were second nature to this intimate family group. Diana was beginning to understand most of the cryptic statements she had been hearing ever since her visits with Charles had brought her closer to the royal family.

In all, it was a very relaxing affair. Diana felt that she and Prince Charles were on a much more solid footing than they had been before. That thought warmed her.

She found time to talk to him later that evening.

"I had no chance to tell you before. I liked your penthouse in Kensington."

He smiled warily. "I thought you might have."

"There wasn't any chance to tell you."

"It did turn out to be a rather abrupt evening."

"Charles, I didn't want it to be like that. But I never thought I had to explain."

"You didn't need to," he said, looking into her eyes. She felt his hand on her wrist. "I *do* understand—now."

She found it hard to select the right words. "I didn't mean to hurt you."

"I wasn't hurt. It takes a lot more than that to wound me."

"I thought you had read my signals correctly, or I might have handled it differently."

"I had read them. I simply decided to act."

She tried to smile, but blushed instead. She could feel her eyes growing hot. "I was wondering if I'd ever see you again, you know."

"You're seeing me right now, aren't you?" His hand tightened on hers.

"You do forgive me?" She looked up at him and found him watching her fondly.

"There's nothing to forgive. I simply had a question that I wanted answered. And now it's answered."

She didn't know quite how he meant that. He was always enigmatic; he had learned to be ambiguous to prevent people from drawing too many conclusions about his thoughts and his desires. All she could do was take it on good faith that he did understand, that he did tolerate her own freakish way of being old-fashioned amidst the new-fashioned social structure.

"I'm becoming very fond of you, Diana," he said a moment later, watching her as he spoke, and then looking purposely away. "But I suppose that's obvious."

"I love to hear you say it anyway." She smiled.

"I'm not alone. Everyone around here loves to have you around."

She couldn't find her tongue. Her face was burning.

"You know I'm leaving for India in a week or so from now. I've a great deal of preliminary work to do. I won't be able to see you next weekend."

"I understand." She understood, but the thought saddened her.

"I'll telephone when I can. That means when I'm in India as well. I don't mind being out of sight, but I don't want to be out of mind."

Silence fell. Diana realized they were holding hands like a couple of schoolchildren. The thought of it gave her a warm glow.

Saturday was another chilly day, with Charles once again out hunting, but back in time to enjoy himself in the evening. The reporters, he told everyone gleefully, were still keeping their vigil, but now all the pressure of the "birthday announcement" had been relaxed.

The non-announcement of the non-engagement had made all the headlines. Diana found it interesting to see how a great deal of words could be generated by the absence of action. In fact, in skilled hands, a non-happening could take precedence over a happening that might actually be much more important. It all depended on what kind of focus the press wanted.

Diana had a pleasant chat with her grandmother, Lady Fermoy, and the Queen Mother in the afternoon.

"Charles was quite proud of the way you managed to elude the press," the Queen Mother said. "He thinks you're quite something."

Diana found herself blushing again. "It's a trick I can only use once."

"You'll think of something else," Diana's grandmother said. "I've never seen them so persistent."

"You'd think they had finally found someone they could believe in," the Queen Mother said. She exchanged a glance with Lady Fermoy.

"I suppose they want me to wear that Liberty skirt again so they can put me all over the front pages," Diana said ruefully.

On Sunday, Charles had one of the security guards bring Diana's new Mini Metro up from the garage where it was locked. The driver used a back road that was out of sight of the reporters at the front gate.

Diana packed and took her bag down to the car, said goodbye to Charles, and got in. One of the Special Branch drivers escorted her out of the estate in a Range Rover all the way to the main road. Diana followed, and at the turn, waved him off and started out on her own.

She found herself dreaming blissfully as she drove along, thinking of Charles. She did not know exactly what he meant by his enigmatic talk of "questions" and "answers," but she could assume that they meant what she wanted them to mean.

Suddenly she realized that a car had pulled up beside her on the highway. She glanced over casually and was astonished to see the reporter who had spotted her at Balmoral Castle. There was another man in the car with him, and the passenger had a camera.

How had they found her out? How had they been able to trace her? Charles had been right. They were everywhere. They had found out about the Mini Metro some way. And they had watched it being driven to Wood Farm for her. Now they were following her to London.

She burst out laughing at the sheer excitement of the chase. If they wanted to race, she would race. Diana had never been a timid driver. Three crackups in her Volkswagen proved that. She loved to drive fast. Now she had a brand-new car, a good car, one that could make speed. She'd show them.

Even though she was breaking in the new car, she decided to throw caution to the winds and give Fleet Street a run for its money.

She pushed the pedal to the floorboard and gunned out along the highway. The Fleet Street car was lost in the distance. But then it came up behind her again. She could see the photographer in the rear seat, positioning himself to get a good picture of her from the rear window.

Whitaker of the *Star* was driving. He got around in front of her somehow. Diana was enjoying the thrill of the chase. The Fleet Street car was three feet in front of her when the photographer looked out the back window and got his shots, straight through the windshield front-on. She was laughing and enjoying every minute of it.

Soon the newsmen had their pictures and the car dropped behind her. Diana resumed her journey at a more normal speed. She felt exhilarated, excited, and happy to be alive after a beautiful weekend.

11

Now that Prince Charles's thirty-second birthday had brought forth no news about an engagement, Fleet Street apparently decided that the news lay in another direction. The expedient was to focus on the romance itself rather than on its official nature. On November 17, the *Sunday Mirror* printed a story that Prince Charles had twice smuggled Lady Diana Spencer aboard the royal train to indulge in secret "love trysts."

These meetings had taken place, the story said, on the nights of November 5 and 6. Diana Spencer's blue Renault had been seen near the train on those nights, the *Mirror* said.

Prince Charles was shown the story several days after it was printed. He was busily preparing for his India trip but turned his attention to it. He had been on the train on November 5, when it had been on a siding at Staverton, but the train had not been there on November 6. He used the royal train to travel from one engagement to another when his schedule was full. The train served as a residence from which to make multiple appointments on a tight schedule.

He was immediately outraged over the publication of this totally false story. The fact was that he was not at all with Diana Spencer on either November 5 or 6. He had been with her on November 4; that was the night of Princess Margaret's birthday party at the Ritz Hotel. Charles met with the Queen. The two of them called in Michael Shea, the Queen's press secretary, and instructed him to write a letter to the editor of the *Sunday Mirror*. The letter, marked NOT FOR PUBLICATION, protested in the strongest possible terms the story and its innuendos. These were, in the words of the letter, "totally false," and the story was a "total fabrication." Shea requested a printed apology in a prominent position at the newspaper's earliest opportunity.

"Darling," Charles told Diana on the telephone, "we're doing all we can to have that story in the *Sunday Mirror* retracted. We don't know if the paper will apologize. I agree it's a messy business, but there's not much else we can do about it."

"I haven't read it. What does it say?"

Charles hesitated. "It says we had a 'love tryst' on the royal train on November 5 and November 6."

"I've never even been on the royal train!" Diana cried.

"I know that," Charles told her soothingly.

"Besides, that was the night after the party. I was tired. I stayed in the apartment."

"There's a claim that your car was seen near the siding."

"My car?"

"The blue Renault."

"That's not *my* car. That's the Spencer car. Anyway, I wasn't using the Renault that week. My Volkswagen was in the repair shop. I hadn't even bought the Metro. I had borrowed my mother's car."

"I can prove you weren't there on November 5, too. I had dinner with three officials of the Duchy of Cornwall."

"How can they print those lies?"

"We'll get it straightened out. Please not to worry."

Charles hung up, unnerved. It was doubly ironic that of all the dozens of women he had taken out it should have been Diana who was accused of flexible morals. He was glad he had warned her. If she had been shown the story by someone else, she would have been much more upset. There was nothing he could do about it now. Besides, he had to prepare for his long trip; he would be leaving shortly after the weekend.

Luckily, he had already arranged with Diana not to see her on the weekend he planned to leave for Delhi. That meant the press would not be on hand to exert pressure on the "love tryst" story. He could make his exit from England with some degree of calm. He had always been able to rise above his relationships with women. Somehow, Diana Spencer was a bit different. He didn't want her to be hurt.

Prince Charles didn't actually mind traveling from one place to another. He rather enjoyed it. He had always traveled well, all his life. Ceremonials were a bore, but he seemed to bear up under them. But this time the three-week period that lay ahead of him seemed to stretch on into eternity.

Once he had landed at Delhi Airport with all the bands playing and the dignitaries out to meet him, he put Diana out of his mind. India was a particularly nostalgic region. Once the pearl in the crown of Great Britain, the area was now an independent group of states, all more or less molded into social units by British planning and sovereignty, and still close to England in tradition and culture.

What was closer to Charles's heart was the fact that his great uncle, Lord Louis Mountbatten, had made his fortune in India and had left his imprint on its culture through his actions during World War II. It was always with a pang that Charles thought of his great uncle, so recently interred.

In fact, Charles had originally planned to take this tour of India in the company of his great uncle, including a trip to Nepal to see Charles's good friend King Birendra. The ghost of "Uncle Dickie" lingered over the impressive ceremonials that greeted Charles upon landing.

It was not until Tuesday night that he had a chance to telephone home. He called Diana first. There was a five-and-a-half-hour difference between Delhi and London time, and it was early morning when he woke her up. But she was waiting to talk to him.

Charles told her what he could about the trip and the ceremonies he was going through. Diana immediately launched into an impassioned attack on the *Sunday Mirror*, which in its recent issue had refused to apologize for the royal train story and, in fact, on November 23 had printed a reply to the Queen's press secretary denying that they had printed anything in error.

"They say they don't publish things wantonly or recklessly," Diana told him, her voice trembling. "The editor says he believes that the original report was true."

"But it's an outright lie!"

"He even says that he doesn't think the story reflects badly on us!"

"That's too much!"

"Can we sue for libel, Charles?"

"Oh, the crown has never sued the press!" Charles was astonished at the suggestion.

"You *won't* sue?" Diana asked.

"There would be a court hearing. No, we couldn't let that happen."

Charles was startled to hear Diana burst into tears as she spoke her next few words. They were so muffled he couldn't tell what she had said.

AP photo

Di-hard fans

MACEDON, Australia — Great Britain's Princess Diana stops to chat with some children at Macedon, where she and Prince Charles visited the town Saturday. The children presented her with flowers, but would not relinquish their sign.

Death toll in tanker explosion ris

"Diana! Please! I'll talk to the Queen! Don't do that."

After a moment or two she regained control of herself and changed the subject. But Charles was infuriated over her emotional breakdown—infuriated at the people who had caused it.

Next day, Charles was present at a reception in the British High Commission in Delhi, where he was chatting with a number of officials and a small group of reporters who had flown along with the royal party from London. Charles was uttering profound assessments of the weather in India, the international situation, and social problems, including the incredible poverty in certain parts of India.

And then, right in the middle of one of the pontifications, he began musing privately. "Diana's a very nice girl, you know."

Several of the reporters turned to him, looking at him with startled surprise. He could see that they were trying to cover their amazement.

Charles realized that he had shifted gears rather abruptly, as it were. And besides, what was he standing around talking about Diana Spencer for?

"All this," he went on, "has been something of a strain for her, you know." He was thinking about the *Sunday Mirror* story. He was also thinking about her demeanor ever since they had begun going out together. "At times," he went on, "it has reduced her to tears."

In a way, Prince Charles was as astonished to hear what he was saying as some of the reporters were. Yet he could not stop now that he had started.

Paul Callan of the *Daily Mirror* commented that he thought that Diana Spencer was coping *very well* under heavy pressure.

"That's kind of you to say so," Charles told Callan. "I must say I think she has been magnificent."

The reporters hemmed and hawed, saying little.

"You know, you must not rush me," he told them after a moment. "What you don't understand is that because a girl stays in the same house overnight, well, it isn't a case of 'Here we go, hooray and whoopee.' It simply cannot be like that. In my position I have to live a rather old-fashioned life. And so do those in my circle."

Stay in the same house? The Palace? Sandringham? Balmoral? "Old-fashioned life?" Harry Arnold of the *Sun* repeated. "Are you talking about marriage? Marriage to Diana Spencer?"

"Gentlemen, I'm talking about life, generally." He smiled. "If only I could live with a girl before marrying her. But I can't. It's all right for chaps like you. You can afford to make a mistake, but I've got to get it right the first time. And if I get it wrong, you will be the first to criticize me in three years' time."

A moment later he was talking about something else not remotely connected with Diana Spencer or marriage. Yet his mind was still centered on Diana. He was thinking about her, in a most unfamiliar context. He knew she was only nineteen years old, virtually completely unworldly. But she was a charming, sweet girl. Could she carry on with him in one of the most difficult pressure spots in the world? Did she have enough strength of character to handle one of the most exalted positions in the social world?

He was thinking of her, he realized with some astonishment, as a possible wife. A wife!

Next stop on Charles's itinerary was a flight over thousands of miles into the snow-capped Himalayas to visit the Kingdom of Nepal. It was here that Prince Charles decided to abandon the party and spend some time alone with himself. He had been through a complicated and very hard year. There were pieces of his life he had to try to sort out.

He went backpacking into the wilds of Annapurna, the

22,000-foot-high mountain in the heart of the world's most isolated region. Accompanied by security men, porters, guides, and the entourage of secretary, press officer, and personal doctor, Prince Charles nevertheless felt freer than he had for many months.

The scenery was absolutely breathtaking. There were trails that wound through lush green valleys and up into the subtropical foliage of the foothills leading to what was called, quite accurately, the Roof of the World.

Charles thought back on his years at school—Gordonstoun, Timbertop—and life in the service when he had been close to nature the same way he was now. Walking at the head of the column of associates, he wore a khaki bush jacket and rough boots and hiking togs.

At night the group sat around a blazing campfire, talking about anything and everything, munching on carp freshly caught in the lakes they passed. Charles even brought along his watercolors. He had not touched paints for years; he never had the time. Now he painted two watercolors of the dramatic mountain views he saw.

And he walked; he walked all the time. He had always prided himself on his physical fitness. It did not desert him now. He was not actually ever tired; he always wanted to go a hundred more paces.

He washed in the mountain streams, and bathed when he could in water that was alternately chilled by the ground and warmed by the sun. He let his beard grow as he had when he was in the service. It was wonderfully relaxing.

In the morning when he awoke, he could see for miles and miles into the clear, bright cold air. It was almost like waking up in a picture window looking out at the most fabulous scenery in the world. And there was the silence, too. It was absolute. Only the murmur of the voices of the men in his company marred the complete silence that surrounded him.

It was during these moments of total peace and tranquillity that he began to sort out the various threads of his life. He had made many mistakes in his relationships in the past few years. He had managed to fall in love with a number of women who did not actually love him enough to take him as he was—along with all the things that went with him.

And so it was of the utmost importance that he try to see how Diana Spencer fitted into the picture. Would she be able to handle the pressures that were too much for many older and more experienced women to withstand? Would she be able to cope with almost anything that came up?

Charles remembered with amusement Diana's innate ability to take the blows of adversity without panicking. That first embarrassment, the photographs of her without her slip on—that could have finished a less durable woman. And the constant harassment by the press—she had almost reveled in trying to beat them at their own game. He remembered her ploy to switch cars and leave a false trail at Coleherne Court to baffle them.

He also remembered with a rueful pang the decisive manner in which Diana had repulsed him when he had made a pass at her in his London hideaway. Not many women had the temerity to turn down the advances of the Prince of Wales. Yet she had. At first he had thought her completely mad. But on thinking it over, he realized that she was showing him something that he had not grasped; the fact that she was serious about him.

That was the question she had answered: the question about her own feelings. She was most certainly in love with him. He had always sensed that; it was a difficult thing to hide. Numbers of women had been in love with him before. He knew how to read them easily enough. But in Diana's case, she backed up her love with a rare strain of no-nonsense strength.

But she had her sensitivity, too. The fact that she was so upset over the newspaper stories about that secret tryst endeared her to him. He knew there was nothing that could be done about the press; it was there to stay and it would always be there. Most of it was not vicious; some of it was.

Diana Spencer could handle them very well. He had seen her in action. She had proved that she could survive almost any assault they could mount against her.

He knew that Kanga and Camilla—his most intimate confidantes—thought the world of her. He knew that his own family group approved of her wholeheartedly. He knew that the Queen Mother was especially attracted to her and Charles had always counted on what his grandmother said and thought. And his mother was close to the Earl Spencer, Diana's father; *she* approved of Diana, too—wholeheartedly.

What was stopping him? Absolutely nothing.

The only question was, would *she* have *him?*

All he had to do was ask.

He came down from the rugged mountain trails with renewed vigor and an entirely new outlook on life. He could see that the members of the royal party were somewhat surprised at the dramatic change in his disposition.

"There's a calm and confidence," one of them told him. "The royal tour seems to be back on the track again."

"It's as if some huge burden was suddenly lifted from your shoulders," another confided in him.

From Pokhara, the party flew back to Katmandu in the Andover jet, piloted by Charles most of the way. In Katmandu, he had dinner in the palace with an old friend of his, the King of Nepal.

Next day Charles piloted the Andover from Katmandu International Airport three thousand miles to Bahrain, with a refueling stop at Oman. There, in Bahrain, with the nucleus of his entourage, including his secretary, press secretary, and detective-bodyguards, he boarded a British Airways scheduled flight for the Seychelles.

Later in the evening of December 14, Prince Charles was once again on British soil at Heathrow Airport. Diana Spencer was not there to greet him. She was too discreet for that. Besides, they had planned it that way on the telephone.

The airport was seething with newsmen. Photographers, journalists, and television crews surged forward to meet him. It was obvious to Charles that the excitement over Diana Spencer had not abated a bit during his trip away to the ends of the earth.

This time he was ready for them all. He hurried along without saying a word, fending off questions with a smile or with a quick quip that meant nothing. An aide rushed out to meet the troupe as they approached the parking area.

"The Queen says she wants to see you as soon as you are free, Your Royal Highness."

Charles nodded. He had a good idea about what she wanted to see him.

He got in the Ford Granada station wagon that was waiting for him. His associates climbed in too. Charles started it up himself. He was so anxious to get it going that he almost killed the engine.

He was back. There were no more days of solitude and tranquility ahead of him. He had a country to serve. And a number of other problems to iron out.

12

Lady Diana Spencer had not been relegated to public obscurity by the absence of Prince Charles, although she had entertained high hopes of suddenly becoming invisible. If anything, the pressure on her intensified.

Her three roommates and her friends at the kindergarten gave her appropriate sympathy for the story in the *Sunday Mirror* about the supposed royal train love tryst. Their help was appreciated, but it really wasn't enough.

Diana did not want to run to the royal family with her woes. She knew it would be difficult to arrange a meeting, even if she wanted it. After her conversation with Charles on the telephone, there had been the Queen's request for a retraction and apology, but nothing had come of that.

She was annoyed generally with the press for the liberties its practitioners could take with the truth, particularly in printing sensational stories that cast public figures in a bad light.

Diana thought about how she could counteract such false stories. She knew that when a statesman wanted to refute an allegation that had been cast against him by a political foe, he called a press conference to make an opposing statement. She could hardly call a press conference; it would only aggravate the situation. She would then be accused of "protesting too much," and find herself even more suspect.

Before she made any move, a savior appeared. Ironically enough, he came to her in the manifestation of a journalist. It was the very man who had first spied her with Charles on the River Dee. One night during Charles's long absence, Diana was stopped in front of Coleherne Court on her return from work. James Whitaker suggested that if she wanted to deny the *Mirror* story, the *Star* would be glad to print her denials in full.

It was a neat way out. If this journalist would print her side of the story, she would not be required to call any press conference or find any other method of getting her story out. She could make her interview a rebuttal of the charges. Trying to ascertain how Prince Charles might view such a procedure, she decided that this time it was up to her and not up to Charles to make a decision.

"I'd welcome the chance to clear this up, Mr. Whitaker," she told him.

She told the facts as clearly as she could. The story appeared in the *Star*, all very favorable for her. It was, in fact, the very first time Lady Diana Spencer had ever given an interview directly to a journalist. Diana had some second thoughts about going out on the limb so deliberately; however, the reaction of the public seemed to be favorable to her. At least, she thought, it took some of the steam out of the original *Mirror* story.

Diana realized that she had not counted on one thing. Now that she had become an established favorite of Prince

Charles, and now that she had been quoted in an exclusive newspaper story, she was now fair game for the entire Fleet Street population. Almost immediately the troops of newsmen following her increased.

"Are you going to marry Prince Charles?" was one question that was frequently asked. "Is it true that the Prince has already asked you to become his wife?"

She forced herself to fend off these personal questions as well as she could. She knew that she could say neither yes nor no to those questions. Stories filled the newspapers about all manner of facts related to Diana Spencer.

"Is the name of your estate pronounced Althrup, Altrup, or Althorp?" one asked her.

"Some of the family pronounce it Altrup. I personally say Althorp. It's all a matter of choice." Her father always said Althorp, too.

Reams and reams of material now appeared about Diana's past. She read it all with a kind of wearied stoicism.

Not all the coverage was sympathetic or done with professional competence. One neighbor at Coleherne Court got into a conversation with her about the press and the way the journalists clamored around her. Diana admitted that it was difficult to make her way about the city.

"The whole thing's got out of control," she said. "It's not so much boring for me but boring for the public seeing my face in the paper every day. I'm not so much bored as miserable. Everywhere I go there's someone there."

The "neighbor" was a free-lance journalist who made good money selling her "private conversation" with Diana to the *Daily Mail*.

The Press Association released a story that twisted what she said into quotations that made her seem to be pining over Prince Charles, that she wished she would be married soon, and that she missed him. When Diana read the story, she realized that the words put into her mouth made her look foolish and childish.

At one point she was astounded to read a letter in *The Times* from her mother, Mrs. Shand Kydd. Diana had no inkling that her mother was going to take the press to task for misquoting her daughter. It made her feel ever more embattled.

By the time she had read what her mother had to say to the press, Diana was despondent. She wished Charles was nearby so she could confide in him. Telephoning halfway across the world was no way to establish intimate communication. She took to staying in the apartment at night, trying to keep a stiff upper lip.

"It's all coming apart," she confessed to her roommates one night toward the end of Charles's trip to India. "I guess I've made a terrible fool of myself."

Carolyn shook her head. "Don't let it bother you that much. You've been subjected to a tremendous strain. How could you be expected to do it all right?"

Diana straightened. "I've got to do it right," she said. "If I don't, how can I be expected to survive the press? They'll always be there."

"You've got to change your tactics," Carolyn told her. "You've got to stop talking to the press."

"How can I do that?"

"You're too honest," Virginia suggested. "Instead of telling them everything they want to know, you've got to protect yourself—and Prince Charles."

"Don't talk so much," suggested Anne. "Just keep your mouth shut whenever they ask a question about your feelings for His Royal Highness, or about him."

"I agree with Anne," said Carolyn. "Simply don't tell them *everything*."

"It's difficult for me to lie," Diana observed.

"All right," said Carolyn. "We know that. And you shouldn't lie. But you don't have to tell them the whole story. Keep something back."

"But then they'll twist what I *do* say—"

"The less they have to go on, the less they'll be able to twist it," Anne said. "Even that reporter who was talking to us the other afternoon said that."

Diana sat up straight. "What reporter?"

Anne flushed. "Well, one of those journalists did come up here. He's very nice. An older man. The one who saw you in Scotland."

Diana was stunned. What right had reporters to talk to her intimate friends?

"He was pretty hard on us," Carolyn admitted. "He told us that we weren't helping you enough. That we weren't giving you enough protection."

Diana knew that he had printed her retraction of the love-tryst story.

"He said the whole business was getting out of hand," Anne said. "And he told us that you'd lose Prince Charles—he called him His Royal Highness—if you didn't do a better job of bottling up your feelings about him."

Diana flushed with anger. "What did he get out of you? That was just a ploy to make you talk!"

"No, Diana," said Virginia. "Honestly. He was trying to be helpful. He wants you to succeed."

"Don't get mad at him," Carolyn told her. "The best thing for you to do is to act as if nothing had happened. Treat them the same way you have been treating them. But don't tell them anything that's important."

Diana's anger had slowly dwindled. "Actually, it's like a game, isn't it? Before the pressure was on it was simply a matter of keeping out of sight. Now I've got to keep in sight but not say anything."

"Who says you have to keep in sight?" Carolyn asked.

"I can't use that marvelous trick when I exchanged the Volkswagen for a Mini Metro again!"

"No, but there are variations on that," Carolyn pointed out.

"You've got to shake them when you go down to meet Charles on his return from India."

"We've decided it's too risky. There'll be such a crush. I'm not going at all."

"When will you be seeing him?"

Diana told them and they sat there planning what to do.

Several days after Prince Charles had returned, Diana, on a routine shopping tour, was followed in her car by a journalist and a photographer. They had learned, they told her, that the *Times* was reserving a whole page of its Friday edition to announce the engagement of Lady Diana Spencer to Prince Charles. Was it true?

Diana was appalled. She did not know what to say. She knew that the statement could be a ploy to trick her into a denial—which would be a story in itself—or some kind of riposte that would actually force her to name the date.

But there wasn't any date; there wasn't any engagement.

On the other hand, if the *Times* did print the story, it would certainly seal her doom. She would go the way of Princess Marie-Astrid of the Netherlands. Once the engagement was announced prematurely, she knew Charles would immediately break it off with her.

"Please," she told the newsmen. "Check your information more thoroughly."

"If you won't deny the fact, I'll have to write my story of your engagement," the journalist said.

"I can't explain to you. There is a very difficult situation. I want to help, but I must not. You have to understand how hard this is for me."

"Look. It's obvious to me that you haven't denied the

announcement. I'm going ahead with the story. But I do wish you'd substantiate it."

She couldn't substantiate it; she couldn't deny it. She was close to tears. "You'll make yourself look the fool if you print that story."

"No more so than the *Times*." He smiled.

Diana went over in her mind the conversation she had had with her roommates. In spite of the fact that she was so near tears, she did not lose her mental composure. She said nothing either to confirm or deny; she did, in fact, lead him over other paths, giving him some vague information that he could use in a story.

After about twenty minutes he looked up. "All right. I won't use the story about the engagement."

Diana closed her eyes in relief. "Good. People have once again got excited too soon."

With that the interview ended.

Two days later Diana arose in the morning early, glanced out the window, and saw several members of the Fleet Street Day Watch in a car across the street. She smiled and took the suitcase she had packed the night before and walked out of the apartment to put it in the back seat of her red Mini Metro. Moments later she returned, carrying a green jacket and a pair of green Wellington boots. She put those inside the car next to the suitcase.

Out of the corner of her eye she saw the men in the car sit up. It was obvious to her that they were thinking she was off to visit Prince Charles at Balmoral. He had arrived in London but had disappeared; he was said to be in Scotland.

Diana went back into the apartment and put on a scruffy old coat that she sometimes used to make short walking trips to the local shops.

"Five minutes," she told Carolyn.

She went down, opened the door, and walked slowly toward Earl's Court Road. She could see that the journalists in the car were watching; they did not follow. They deduced that she was making a last-minute purchase before returning to dress up and then get in the car to drive off.

Diana hurried along the sidewalk once she was out of sight of the reporters. Four and a half minutes later she was standing on the corner around the block. A cab came up with Carolyn in it. She got out, handed Diana another suitcase with her things in it, and Diana got inside, giving the cabby directions to take her to Heathrow.

At Heathrow she checked quickly to see if she had been spotted, but for once there were not the usual number of journalists manning the lines. The plan seemed to be working out well. Once at Dyce Airport, she was met by one of Charles's detectives, who drove her quickly, not to Balmoral Castle but to Birkhall, the home of the Queen Mother.

When Diana saw Charles for the first time in several weeks, she was surprised at his own expression of open affection and delight. He was not a demonstrative man, but when she came into the room, he hugged her tightly and kissed her quickly but effectively. She sensed immediately that things were on quite a different level than they had been before.

She leaned back and looked up at him. "You've been outdoors a lot. You look wonderful!"

"Yes," he admitted. "It was something I needed."

"I'm glad to have you back."

"You've been surviving."

"But only surviving," Diana said with a smile.

Diana unpacked her things and chatted with the Queen Mother, who embraced her, and her grandmother, who kissed her affectionately, and then dressed in her sweater and slacks and gumboots and found Charles. They had tea, over which they gazed at one another with surprised delight. Diana was quite impressed—Charles's typical moodiness and remoteness had changed into something quite rare and unexpected: an almost palpable attachment. There was something electric in the air between them.

They walked outside under the trees, taking a breath of fresh air. Diana sighed in the bright sunshine, breathing in the smell of the trees and the grass. The birds were singing and the breeze was moving the leaves in the trees.

Charles turned to her and took her hand. "You're looking lovelier than ever."

She blushed charmingly. "Thank you."

"I read the interview you gave about the royal train mess."

She could not read his expression. He was a most difficult man to fathom. Why bring up this mundane thing now?

"I thought you handled it very well. In a way, you made yourself much more attractive to the public." He grinned. "And to me!" He ruffled her hair and embraced her. She held her breath, feeling the strong muscles of his lithe body.

"I didn't know whether or not I should have done it that way," she confessed.

"It was a bold step, but it was right."

Diana sighed. "It opened the floodgates. I haven't had a moment's rest since then."

"That's the way it works. Once you establish yourself as a person, you become an object of interest. You can't hide anymore."

"I know that now."

"Do you want to hide?"

"No."

They were looking into one another's eyes. Charles pressed her closely and kissed her firmly. They stood there a long time in the woods, enjoying the touch of their bodies and listening to the sounds of the woods.

They began walking again, arm in arm. Diana felt the overwhelming warmth of intimacy; her thoughts soared romantically into the heavens. He began telling her about the exalted experience of tramping through the wilderness at the Roof of the World. She told him about the reporters watching her outside Coleherne Court and the way she and her roommates had handled her departure that morning. She felt there was little comparison between the two exchanges, but he enjoyed her story and laughed long and hard at it.

"We'll both be doing a lot more of that in the future," he told her, gripping her hand.

For once, the news of their meeting at Birkhall did not leak out. The public had not the slightest inkling that they were there together. Next morning the two of them were able to go fishing without the prying eyes of the public. Charles began to teach Diana how to cast properly. They came back with a few fish—not many for a day's work—but their spirits were revived and they were reveling in the secluded peace and quiet about them.

Diana loved the long evenings by the fire as they sat about chatting with the Queen Mother and Diana's grandmother. Charles detested cards, but the Queen Mother loved to play. When they weren't fishing or hiking around the trails nearby, they were driving about the private roads or walking around Birkhall.

The swift-moving moments following their reunion had all but swept Diana off her feet. Her intimacy with Charles was now an established thing. The way was open for the next move—and that was on Charles's part. On the long strolls through the Scots woods, Diana felt completely at one with Charles. She could almost swear he loved her. But he did not talk about it.

For all their newfound intimacy and for all Charles's tranquillity and decisiveness, Diana found herself no nearer to being engaged than she had been the first time they had gone fishing at Balmoral. Once or twice it seemed almost as if Charles were struggling for the words to ask her to marry him; but they never came.

Yet, at the same time, some of his statements became inexorably bound up with a future marriage.

"We'll be getting down to Highgrove soon," he said once. "Have you been thinking about the furnishings in the nursery?"

Diana blinked. "Not really. There's plenty of time for that."

She stared at him blankly. What did he mean? Was he planning for children? If he was, why didn't he let her in on it? Did he want her expertise on nursery furnishing *for someone else?*

Obviously not.

Another time he burst out with a question that seemed to intrude on an otherwise simple exchange of banalities.

"Do you like summer weddings or spring weddings best?"

She was somewhat jarred. "I never gave it a thought." She had, of course, but she would not let him know that. Immediately she softened that with, "I suppose it all depends on the circumstances."

Yes, she thought. What *were* the circumstances? If he proposed now, they could be married in the spring. Was that what he wanted? Was he backing that up with Plan B—a summer wedding, if he didn't get around to proposing until spring?

But he had turned to her, staring.

She flushed. "I mean, of course, it depends on the family obligations of the people being married. For example, who's being married?"

"Well, if you have to ask—" he mumbled.

She was embarrassed and chagrined. He still had not

answered the question or put the conversation into the proper focus.

Suddenly he laughed and the tension was broken. "That's not an honest question, is it?"

"No!" she snapped, relieved but angry.

"Sorry." His thoughts had drifted far off again.

The Queen Mother drew her aside one evening. "I think it's been very good for Charles to have been able to see you here. I've loved having you."

"Thank you," Diana said. "You know how I feel about Birkhall. It's like a home away from home for me—with my grandmother here with you."

"Charles looks well, doesn't he?" she observed vaguely. "I do wish I knew how he felt about things." She darted a glance at Diana. "Particularly about you."

Diana sighed. "So do I."

Lady Fermoy had joined them. "Then I take it that nothing has been said."

Diana shrugged.

"Well, I do wish he'd get on with it," the Queen Mother said in a sprightly tone. "I tell you, if he doesn't, I'm going to do something about it."

Diana shook her head. "Please don't. It's all very delicate."

"Oh, I know!" she snapped. "Sometimes I simply don't understand any of them!" She was obviously talking about the Windsors. Diana giggled.

"It's been wonderful having you," Lady Fermoy told Diana, hugging her and kissing her. The Queen Mother left the room and grandmother and granddaughter were alone together.

"Men!" said Lady Fermoy.

"But he's the heir apparent!" Diana protested.

"He'll be an old bachelor if he doesn't move!"

"I think he likes me."

"It isn't enough!"

"I can wait."

"You're young," said Lady Fermoy. "Just a child. Why doesn't he get on with it?"

"Don't *do* anything, Grandma! And please don't let the Queen Mum do anything. This is all very sensitive."

Lady Fermoy made a sound under her breath, but then smiled again, and the conversation moved away from Charles.

It was all over on Sunday afternoon. Diana flew back to London. She got past the passenger crush at Heathrow and took a cab home to Coleherne Court. She was greeted by several reporters at her door.

"Have a nice holiday?"

"Lovely," she told them noncommittally.

13

Prince Charles was a puzzled man. During those beautiful days at Birkhall he had been on the verge of proposing to Diana Spencer a number of times. But something had always held him back. Odd, because he had made up his mind before returning to England to ask her to marry him.

By the time Diana was packing to go back to London, he had realized it was too late to make a formal proposal in Scotland. It would look a bit drab and prefabricated. But there was something bothering him about the whole business. He had a feeling of being manipulated. There were wheels within wheels, as the saying went; a riddle wrapped in a mystery inside an enigma.

He knew too that the Queen was after him. She rarely hovered over him anymore. But since he had returned from India, she had been putting out all sorts of signals that she wanted to sit down with him and talk.

The talk would be about marriage; of that he was absolutely certain. He had purposely fallen in with the Queen Mother's plans to spend that time at Birkhall with Diana. And it was set up beautifully for a proposal. Yet he could feel invisible chains binding him, strings being pulled, manipulations behind the scenes.

He wanted to see Diana again immediately. Perhaps they could straighten things out before Christmas. By that time he would be obligated to speak to the Queen and Prince Philip. If he could get things sorted out by then . . .

He called Camilla Parker-Bowles and found that she would be happy to have the two of them over any time Charles wanted. She was anxious to hear about his trip to India; mostly she wanted to hear about Diana—and to see her.

Christmas was rapidly approaching. The Prince of Wales was chagrined to read in the newspapers that an announcement of a coming royal wedding was imminent. The rumor mills were busy grinding out miles of material that was based strictly on speculation. Fleet Street had picked up the vibrations, of course; every day there were stories about a Christmas announcement. These rumors were based on the fact that every year the Queen broadcast a traditional Christmas Day message to the nation—that included all the overseas possessions and protectorates of the Crown.

Things were at this stage in the press when Charles and Diana spent the evening at Allington at the Parker-Bowleses' home.

"There's simply no way of putting them down," Charles sighed when the subject of the so-called announcement came up during dinner.

"It's ridiculous," said Parker-Bowles. "Are the editors mad, or simply thick-headed? The Queen's Christmas Day talk has already been recorded. Why, it must be recorded at least two weeks in advance of its broadcast throughout the United Kingdom!"

"I suppose the press loves to keep people guessing," Camilla observed.

"It's simply a matter of logistics," Parker-Bowles went on. "It takes days for the tapes and films to be sent out to all parts of the Commonwealth in the heavy pressure of the Christmas mail rush."

"Besides," Camilla ventured, "how could you keep the fact a secret? Someone would certainly play out the message ahead of time and let the news out prematurely."

"Totally illogical," Parker-Bowles murmured, shaking his head. "Anyway, such a message would be too important to combine with a Christmas Day message. It would obviously be a separate statement."

When Charles glanced over at Diana to see how she was taking all this, he found her toying with her food, a bit distracted. He glanced at Camilla and found her studying him. By now even Parker-Bowles was silent. An odd quiet settled over the dinner table.

Afterward, Charles found conversation hard going. There was not the usual rapport in the friendly confines of the Parker-Bowles home. Charles and Parker-Bowles were usually talking about hunting and fishing or other sports; Camilla and Diana found it easy to chat with one another, in spite of their differences in age.

But tonight it was different.

"Well," Charles suddenly said. "I've simply got to get back to Allibar."

Diana glanced across at him with a look. It was an odd thing to say. "I'm sure he's missed you, Charles," she said wryly.

Parker-Bowles laughed.

Charles looked up, frowning. "Did I miss something?"

"Not yet," Camilla said rather flatly. "But you might."

Charles blinked. "I'm sorry. My thoughts were wandering." He took a deep breath. "I've got a lot on my mind."

"Indeed. Affairs of state?"

"I suppose you could call it that. I don't know, when we get together for Christmas holidays at the castle, it's always a pretty tightly controlled family situation."

"Everything is all right, isn't it?" Camilla asked, her face alert.

"Fine," said Charles. "I was thinking about Christmas and New Year, and all that."

"Oh."

No, Charles thought. It wasn't Christmas and New Year. He was thinking about Diana. But he couldn't say it.

Camilla cast a sidelong glance at Diana, and turned to Charles. "Allibar surely does miss you, Prince Charles. After all, it's almost as if you were married."

"Married?" Charles looked up again. He was feeling uncomfortable vibrations from Camilla.

"To your horse," Camilla went on blandly. "Isn't it pretty much like marriage, when you love Allibar and put all your faith in him when you race?"

Charles could feel those invisible strings again. "I hadn't thought about marriage in those terms."

"How exactly *do* you think about marriage?" Camilla asked carefully.

Charles leaned back in the chair, stretching a bit, luxuriating in front of the fireplace. "A lifelong devotion, thoroughgoing love, a shared lifetime."

"Very nicely put," said Parker-Bowles happily.

"Your instincts are right," said Camilla. "I'm surprised you don't believe in it."

"Who said I didn't believe in it?"

"No one *said* it. Your actions say it."

"I suppose so."

"You've been ten years at least acting out your disdain of marriage."

"Oh, come now!" Charles was rattled. "Besides, how do you know?"

"The facts speak for themselves."

"No. How do you know what my private thoughts are? How do you know even if I've asked anyone?"

Diana was pale. She seemed afraid to look at Camilla, who was now moving in for the kill. Charles could feel it in the air.

"I don't know, of course. But so far—"

"How does a man ever know how he'll be treated when he does ask?" Charles wondered, frowning at the fire.

"He doesn't," Camilla admitted.

"How do I know, for example, what might happen if I were to ask Diana here to marry me—or anyone else, for that matter?"

Diana's face was on fire. She could find nothing to say.

"Does *she* even know how she would answer?" Charles went on, warming to his theme.

"But she does know, Charles," Diana said in a small voice.

Charles drew back quickly. "What would she say?" He turned to her, their eyes meeting. Everything had suddenly got into the third person. In a way, it seemed a bad omen. But he couldn't change it now.

"She hasn't been asked," Diana retorted softly.

"But if she were?"

"Perhaps if she were, the man who asked her would find out."

Charles absorbed that blow easily. "It's definitely not the most agreeable lifestyle on earth," he observed. "Being that kind of wife."

"There's always the press," Charles reminded her.

"I know most of them already," Diana said.

"You see? Already she's given up the idea completely." Charles found himself laughing.

"Oh, I like some of them. They're delightful chaps."

"If I were to ask her, she would have to live with them around the rest of her life."

"She might be able to accomplish that."

Charles had sunk deep in thought. "If a man were to ask her to marry him, what would be her main hope, do you think?"

"She would hope that he would not wait until he was an old man to ask."

After the laughter subsided, the talk drifted off to hunting. Charles was damned if he was going to go back to romance again that night. But as he continued to talk, he continued to think.

In spite of the good-natured repartee, with that rather obvious element of malicious amusement injected by Camilla, whom he had always considered a good friend, Diana had artfully succeeded in not answering Charles's main question. He had no idea whether or not she would accept him. She could be playing a game, he knew. She was young. Maybe she had no desire to settle down yet.

The evening ended early and nothing was decided. Charles began planning his next move carefully. He would see Diana just before Christmas at Windsor Castle, and *then* he would ask her. He could tell the Queen then and everything would be settled.

But once again Charles could feel the manipulation of strings somewhere out of sight. Even though this time he knew the frustration of his plans was simply due to fate, he seemed entrapped. Diana caught the flu and told him she couldn't possibly be with him during Christmas.

She went home to Althorp and stayed in bed over the holidays. He talked to her on the phone, but nothing moved forward at all.

Prince Charles knew that he would be in for a long session with the members of his family during the Christmas holidays. Of all the royal residences, the Queen preferred Windsor. She had spent most of her crucial wartime years growing up there. She had made it into the most private of her residences, the one she most liked to call home.

Charles loved Windsor, too. It had been a royal residence since the days of the Norman Conquest. William the Conqueror acquired the land as a hunting preserve, and replaced a wooden enclosure by a stone wall. The site of the present castle was established by Edward II, who built a structure to form a meeting place for the newly established order of Knights of the Garter—whose motto is: *"Honi soit qui mal y pense,"* as every schoolchild knows. "Evil he who evil thinks." Edward selected the spot because legend had it that it was the site where King Arthur used to sit surrounded by his Knights of the Round Table in fabulous Camelot.

At this epicenter of legend, reverence, and history, the royal family always settled down for Britain's most beloved holiday—Christmas. Psychologically and psychically, this would be the absolutely right time for the Queen to explore the subject of Charles's private life.

Charles knew from the talk around him that the Queen had made her feelings known to the staff that she was going to get to the bottom of Charles's marriage plans. "Even I don't know what's going on!" she told them.

Not only the Queen was displeased. Prince Philip, who rarely mixed in with intimate details of his family's lifestyles, had made the remark that Charles was simply running after one girl after another with no seeming interest in any one of them. "He'd better get on with it soon, or there won't be any of them left for him."

In the beautifully appointed sitting room, Charles finally met with them. He felt as if he were present at an inquisition of sorts, although he did not express it to them that way. But he was uncomfortable.

The first question to come up was what his intentions were toward Diana Spencer. Were they serious?

"I'm very serious about her. She's a simply superb young woman. I'm quite struck by her decency and good character."

"But, don't you see, Charles, that's not quite enough!"

Charles frowned. "Not enough?"

"Have you finally made up your mind to make a positive move?" his father asked him.

"Certainly I have made up my mind," Charles said.

"I'm happy to hear that," said the Queen. "But once again, that isn't really enough."

"You must *act*," said his father.

Charles sighed. "I've only known her for two months. Since September."

"You've known her since she was born!" said the Queen Mother.

"Well, of course, but—"

Prince Philip cleared his throat. "Certainly you've had quite enough time to sow your wild oats, as they used to say. You've been playing the field as much as anyone of your age. But, Charles, you're thirty-two years of age!"

Charles bit his lip. "But—"

"It's time to get this thing settled! Do you know what your feelings are toward her?"

"Of course! I'm sure of *my* feelings."

"Then that's all there is to it," said the Queen triumphantly. "It's all settled."

"How can it be settled, when I'm not sure about her feelings?"

"Oh, Charles! Really! You've been taking her out for weeks now. Can't you tell?"

"I don't know *completely* how she feels about me. About

being—well—married to me. I've more or less asked her, you know. I haven't really been just sitting around!" He was speaking more loudly now.

"Did she turn you down?" the Queen Mother asked.

"No. But at the same time, she didn't really say yes."

"Well, you're simply going to have to get a definite commitment," said the Queen.

"Yes," said Charles. "What I don't want is for her to feel trapped." He was thinking of Anna Wallace. He had asked her, and she had turned him down. She had felt trapped, he knew that.

"What you don't want is a repetition of your last affair," growled his father. "I can appreciate that. You were badly burned. You don't want to look the fool if Diana does decide against you."

"She would hardly do that," the Queen Mother interposed.

Prince Philip shrugged and dropped out of the conversation.

Charles took his cue from his father's intervention. "What I need is very simple. I need some time to sit down quietly with Diana and discuss the matter. I want to leave it up to her and let her decide how she feels."

"You must get her to say yes or no," pleaded the Queen.

"Yes," Charles said.

"What kind of perfect setting do you need in order to bring this thing off?"

"I have to create the proper mood. It's a delicate subject."

"Granted."

"What I need is a few intimate moments with Diana. I don't want the press, the public, and the staff around."

"You had that at Birkhall."

"What exactly *do* you want?" Prince Philip asked.

"I want Diana invited over to Sandringham for the New Year. She'll be recovered from the flu by then. In the seclusion of Sandringham, I'll be able to talk to her quietly. It's home to her, you know."

"That's the answer, then." Prince Philip turned to the Queen, then back to Charles. "But this time, you must not linger too long over the decision. You must bring this thing to a close."

Charles sat there subdued.

The Queen said, "The idea of this romance going on for another year is intolerable for everyone concerned!"

The Queen had spoken. It was a royal command.

After the meeting, Prince Charles telephoned Diana. "You're to come to Sandringham for the New Year, love," he told her.

"I'll be there," she said in a faint voice. She sounded very much under the weather.

Charles sat there after he had hung up. His hands were damp. He felt as if he had been run through the gauntlet.

Merry Christmas and a Happy New Year, he thought.

After the Christmas holidays, the royal family moved over to Sandringham to enjoy the balance of the year-end celebrations. Charles kept in continual touch with Diana by telephone. She was slow in her recovery. He kept reminding her that she still had an open invitation for the New Year.

After its frustration over the non-announcement of the engagement during the Christmas Message of the Queen, the press pulled out all stops during the week between Christmas and New Year's and descended on Sandringham with a vengeance. Sandringham was more remote from London than Windsor Castle, but that did not stop the Fleet Street mob.

As the cavalcade of the royal family pulled into Sandringham, they were appalled to discover an enormous crowd of journalists and photographers—a mob unlike anything they had ever seen there before.

Even the pheasant shooting, one of the main reasons why the royal family moved from Windor Castle to Sandringham during the period after Christmas, became almost impossible. The men in the family had to push their way through the crowds even to get into the fields to shoot. It took almost paramilitary operations to get out at all.

Charles was surprised once when they were coming in to the house to hear the Queen shout out at a group of reporters huddled against the gate:

"I wish you would go away!"

Later on, the Queen's press secretary issued a statement that made all the papers. "The Queen has become increasingly angry at what she considers an intrusion of her privacy. This trip to Sandringham has been far worse than any other. Now it seems that some Fleet Street editors think the Queen is fair game, even when she has no official engagements. No member of the royal family can move out of Sandringham without a posse of pressmen surrounding them. They are hanging about the stables, photographing anything that moves!"

Diana told Charles that she was not well enough by New Year to risk the trip to Sandringham. She stayed at Althorp to recuperate completely.

At Sandringham, the reporters were looking for her everywhere. After all, none of the press had seen her with Charles since his trip to India. Was the romance off? A rumor surfaced during the days between Christmas and New Year, much to the annoyance of the royal family, that indeed the romance had cooled.

To make that rumor more believable, Prince Charles appeared more on edge than usual. No one knew that his attitude was caused by the fact that he had been frustrated by Diana's sickness. He found himself snapping at everyone.

On New Year's Day he strolled by a group of photographers hanging around to find anyone they could quote. The paparazzi took pictures and the reporters asked him questions.

When it was all over, Charles turned to them, with a glint of ice in his blue eyes. "I wish you a very happy New Year. I hope your editors have a particularly nasty one."

Then he turned on his heel and stalked away.

"Well," shouted one of them after him, "I don't wish you anything nasty, Sir. Happy New Year!"

Charles halted, turned, and smiled faintly. He had never known how to handle such irrepressible good nature. "That's very kind, thank you."

He walked off, deep in thought.

Charles was appalled when his youngest brother, Prince Edward, decided to get into the act. He came out one morning with a shotgun in his hands ready for the pheasant and hollered to the press:

"Watch out, you might get shot!"

And to give them a good idea of what that might seem like, he unloosed a barrage of buckshot over the heads of a *Daily Mirror* photographer. The pellets were heard to rattle down on the roofs of some of the cars belonging to the scribes.

All in all, it was not a delightful New Year's Day for Prince Charles or Diana Spencer.

14

On Thursday, January 8, 1981, a week after New Year, Diana Spencer was feeling well enough to drive out to Lambourn in Berkshire. Charles was going to ride the steeplechase at Chepstow in February. He wanted to give Allibar his weekly workout.

"I haven't seen you since long before Christmas," he told her.

By now Diana knew her way around Lambourn and the stables and drove down to the private area near the paddock to park her car. Charles was already there; she saw his car and his Special Branch men. Instead of watching him saddle up, she put on her waterproof coat over her thick sweater and pants and went out into the field where she could watch him.

Charles spent about an hour putting Allibar through his paces. It was cold and dismal. Diana did not want to imperil her recovery. She went inside to watch him stable the horse. Charles came over to her.

"How are you feeling, love?"

"Better."

They kissed.

"Nick has invited us for breakfast at his cottage. We'd better go over separately."

Diana got in her red Mini Metro and drove into Lambourn to the brick front of the Gaselee house. The Gaselees lived in a dead-end street. She parked almost in front of the door, just behind Charles's Ford Granada. Charles arrived a few minutes later, puffing along on a battered bicycle he used to get from the stables to the house. He jumped off the cycle and took Diana into the house.

Judy and Nick Gaselee were waiting for them. Diana knew Judy better than Nick; she found him to be a solid horse trainer, and an easy-going, decent man. They were all chatting easily over breakfast when suddenly Charles rose and stared out the curtained window into the street. He moved over to the curtain and pulled it back. There were several more cars in the quiet lane outside the cottage.

"It's those reporters!" he choked out. "They've seen our cars!"

Diana peered over his shoulder, careful to keep out of sight. She could see a carful of men waiting. They had decided to watch for the two of them to come out together. There was no way they could avoid the confrontation. Because the Gaselee house was situated in a dead-end street, if they went out the back door, they would have to come all the way around to get in their cars.

"They want us together," Charles told her. "You go out first. After you've driven away, I'll go out. They're not going to get us both!"

Diana agreed. She grabbed her coat and bag and strode out the door in sweater and slacks. She glanced at the car where the reporters sat. She smiled at them and then got into her car and drove off.

In moments, Charles followed her. As he came out he waved cheerily at the reporters.

"My, my, you are up early this morning, gentlemen," he said with a touch of sarcasm.

And he drove away, entirely separate from Lady Diana.

However, the press had its story. Diana opened the newspaper the next morning to find a big story under a headline:

CHARLES AND DI TOGETHER

Pictures proved the romance was not cooling, said a subhead under photographs of the two of them emerging separately from the Gaselee cottage.

Charles telephoned Diana later the next day.

"Well, you read the papers," he said. "You and I are together again."

"I didn't know we had split up," Diana joked.

"You missed our invitation to Sandringham over New Year's Day. Can you come this weekend?"

"Of course."

"You're going to have to shake them again. We don't want another New Year fiasco. It was dreadful!"

Diana sat down with her roommates and dreamed up another plan, this one involving misinformation—in other words, a plant. The planted idea, the false lead, was that she was going home to Althorp for the weekend.

By now at least one journalist would call each day at the apartment to find out if Diana was going to see Charles. This time, on January 15, Carolyn took the call, and informed the caller that Diana would be going to Althorp for the weekend. On the morning of January 16, Diana came out of the apartment, cheerily waved at the journalists, and climbed into her red Mini Metro.

Within minutes she was headed for Kensington Palace. By now the reporters knew that she sometimes dropped by on her way home to Althorp to see her sister Jane. They left directly for Northampton and Althorp.

Giggling a bit, Diana met her sister at The Barracks, then went down with her and got into a silver Volkswagen Golf that had been placed at her disposal in the parking lot. In the borrowed Golf, she quickly drove up A10 to Norfolk and Sandringham. Already there were dozens of reporters hanging around the gate at the big house.

Diana passed them up. Entering Sandringham through a back road, she avoided them all and parked just outside the main house. The journalists had begun to thin out just a bit. The lack of news from Sandringham had deterred some editors from spending big money to keep their corps in strength on the wait. Most of them were out after other game.

Prince Charles was busy shooting pheasants and taking care of other business. Actually, Diana felt that she was being virtually ignored. They did sit down once or twice to chat, but it was almost a business-as-usual weekend.

On Sunday, Charles climbed into his own car and drove past the two dozen journalists stationed at the front gate. They immediately got into their cars and followed him, guessing hopefully that he might be going to keep a rendez-vous with Diana.

Instead, Charles led them to the dog kennels on the estate. He got out his golden Labrador retriever Harvey and fed him chunks of meat. He posed with Harvey and the paparazzi took man-and-dog pictures, wondering how in the world they could ever justify their expenses to their bosses for these shots.

Meanwhile, Diana, their real target, was walking quickly out a side door to climb into the silver Volkswagen Golf she had borrowed in London. She got into it, started it up, and drove back to London, arriving by noon.

To keep up the pretense of her unseen presence, the

royal family ate lunch at the King's Head, a local pub. On the way in, Princess Anne, who never in her life had been able to get on well with reporters, peered out of her car and laughed at them to rub it in.

"She's gone, you know."

They all knew about whom she was talking.

After lunch Prince Charles strolled by a group of reporters waiting outside. He paused and seemed to be in a joking mood. After a few inconsequential remarks, he looked over his shoulder at the pub.

"There's no one here. I wish you'd all go away."

Within days, Diana was scheduled to go to Klosters with Prince Charles for a ten-day holiday. Several days before their departure on January 23, Diana called Charles.

"Darling, I'm not going to Klosters."

Charles said nothing for a moment.

"I'm going to Australia."

"Australia?" Charles repeated, slightly stunned.

"I'm going to see my mother," Diana said quietly. "It's been a hectic pace. I want a rest."

Charles hesitated. "I see. And Klosters is definitely out?"

"Too many paparazzi. Too many people." And too many pictures of Charles and Lady Sarah Spencer coming out of the same door she would be coming out of.

"Oh," said Charles. "I'm sorry." He meant it.

"There are too many ifs in this situation. You understand?"

"Yes, I—"

She never heard what he said. There were tears in her eyes as she hung up.

The Klosters decision had been a hard one to make. There were two primary considerations that had finally forced her hand.

First, she was becoming increasingly harassed by the pressure of the media. She had been able to handle very special problems involved in her daily dealings with the press, but after three meetings with Charles, she had begun to weary of the constant battle of wits. She knew that if she accompanied him to Klosters, neither of them would get any rest. It was best she stay home.

Secondly, she was becoming more aware of the cat-and-mouse game in which she was involved with the Prince of Wales. To the outsider, it might seem that she was the front runner in the Prince Charles sweepstakes. To her, she really was in the dark as to his general motives. She *thought* he was serious; she really could not tell. At one moment he seemed to proceed as if the engagement was simply a matter of a few days more until it was finalized: at another he acted as if they were just good friends.

Diana Spencer needed time to unwind, to think it out. She might even turn him down if he asked. She did not really know what to do. There were considerations in becoming Her Royal Highness that she had not yet explored. She needed respite.

Yet when Charles finally flew to Klosters, Diana felt depressed and out of it. It was even worse when she saw Prince Charles on the television news and in the newspapers preparing to tackle the slopes with Patti Palmer Tomkinson, a skiing companion who loved the slopes as much as Charles did. Even though Diana knew Patti was the wife of the man who owned the chalet where Charles stayed, she was still unhappy. She wondered what the press would make out of Charles's appearance without Diana Spencer. Oddly enough, there seemed to be little concern or interest.

Diana's mother was most excited about being able to be with her daughter. She wrote enthusiastic letters, telling Diana what to wear, and what to expect Down Under. The one thing she did not discuss was Charles and Diana. She knew what would be on her daughter's mind when they met.

Charles called almost every night from Switzerland.

"I miss you, love," he told her immediately. "I'm sorry you opted out of the trip. It's lovely on the slopes."

"I wanted to ski, too," Diana admitted. "But I do have to think about things. And I'm tired of dodging the press."

"Actually, there aren't too many of them here," Charles said, a bit remotely. "I guess they want to see you and not me."

Diana giggled. "You know that's not true."

"But it *is* true!" After a brief hesitation, he continued: "Have you decided about going to Australia?"

"I'm going," she told him. "I've discussed it with Mother. She wants me to get away for a while and rest. I'm going down there to stay with her and my stepfather."

"Good. There are lots of things you should be thinking about. Australia's the best place to do it. I love the country! I went to school there, you know."

"Of course I know. I know everything about you!"

"That's probably why you're going off to Australia." He laughed.

"Seriously, I do have to rest. Also I want to talk to Mother. I really haven't been as close to her in these past few months as I should have been."

"Don't scold yourself," he advised soberly. "She's been close to the royal family all her life. She should have a good grasp of the problem."

Diana frowned. What was Charles saying? Was he saying that she should explore the advantages and disadvantages of being Her Royal Highness during her visit to Australia? If he meant that, did he mean the engagement might be a thing of the future? Or was he still playing a game and not saying anything?

"Oh, I don't know what we'll be talking about," Diana said lightly.

"Being close to the throne can prove an awful responsibility," Charles went on, ignoring her comment. "You do have to think about it carefully. I know you will. You're a very careful person."

"Except in my driving!" Diana laughed. "Oh, Charles, I do wish I'd come with you! I'd love to zoom down the slopes."

"It was your decision not to come," he reminded her in a cool tone.

"I couldn't help but think of those photographers. You know, you coming out of the royal chalet with Sarah three years ago. They'd take pictures of us coming out now. And there would be nastier stories than the royal train incident."

"Perhaps you're right." Charles sighed. "That's what I mean about the future. You do have to think it all out in your own mind, darling."

He seemed to be unable to leave the subject.

"In the end it may prove to be too awful to face. If you decide that, I won't be able to blame you at all. You have learned what you must go through."

Diana didn't know quite what to say.

"I'm going to enter a long-distance, cross-country race tomorrow," he told her after some more conversation.

"Oh, I hope you win!"

In fact, he did win a prize in the race. He told her about it a few nights later. He did not return to the subject of her Australian trip and her mental attitude toward royalty.

Diana gathered her things together for the proposed two-week visit to Australia and purchased her tickets. She was scheduled to leave on February 6, a Friday. She was looking forward to the change of scenery and the absence of press pressure.

Diana continued working at the kindergarten. The media

kept constant surveillance on her, but there were fewer requests for interviews now. When Prince Charles returned from Klosters on February 2, several reporters tagged along after Diana to be on hand if she met him. The two of them did not meet, realizing what a crush it would be and how difficult it would be to keep the press from bothering them.

"Are you going to see him before you leave?" Virginia asked her the night Charles returned.

Diana smiled. "I simply don't know."

"He does keep you hanging by your thumbs," said Carolyn.

"He's very busy. Besides, he knows I'm busy getting everything ready for my flight."

Charles did telephone. Diana answered it herself.

"Are you packed already?" he asked in a cheerful tone.

"Yes. I'm leaving Friday." She hesitated, thinking she sounded as if she were simply prattling on about nothing. "So I'll be seeing you about the middle of February."

"No you won't," he told her.

She could feel herself begin to tremble.

"You're coming over for a farewell party at the palace." Charles paused. "Tomorrow night. Wednesday. I thought it best to celebrate your leaving two nights before your flight."

"Oh, that's nice of you, Charles!"

"Be here at eight."

Diana finished up at the kindergarten on Wednesday and went straight to Coleherne Court. There she rested for a time and then got into a long evening gown that she thought would be appropriate for the occasion. She had been to Charles's apartment at Buckingham Palace before, but never for dinner. She felt it was a semiformal occasion, even though it was simply a dinner between friends.

She chose a small evening bag to carry, and tried out one of her warm coats. There was a nip in the February air. She peered out the window to see if the press was covering the entrance, but she could see no one there. It was the middle of the week; Fleet Street was apparently nodding.

By now her roommates were in the house, preparing supper and eating together. Diana presented herself to them, and one by one they suggested minute changes in her attire and makeup. Finally she was ready to go. For some reason she felt almost faint; it was the excitement. Strange, after all she had gone through with Prince Charles that she should feel heady over going to supper with him in his apartment!

She got into her red Mini Metro and drove along Old Brompton Road directly over to the Buckingham Palace gate next to Royal Green Park. The security guard there, who had obviously been alerted to her appearance, waved her right through. Beyond the wrought-iron gate archway there was a small parking lot; there her distinctive car could be hidden from prying eyes.

Glancing around hurriedly, Diana made sure no one was watching her through the iron railing standing between the palace grounds and the public walkway outside. Clutching her bag in her hand, she hurried across to the billiard-room entrance to the palace. A footman in red waistcoat with buttons of brass opened the door for her.

She was inside the palace, with its red-carpeted corridors and its heavy mahogany doors. She was aware of the heavy paintings hanging on the walls, one depicting Elizabeth II's coronation, among others. She was conducted along a scarlet corridor past busts of Victoria, Albert, Edward VII, and others she did not recognize. She was led past an inner courtyard into the Prince of Wales's corner of the palace.

Immediately, she was ushered into the elevator to the second floor, where she walked down a red-carpeted corridor made Christmasy by green walls and lined with lighted display cases. On the right she came to Charles's suite—the Prince of Wales's rooms. She was led past the first room, the luggage room, to the second room of the three-room suite.

This was Prince Charles's most private office. A brown, rather somber room, it contained a large work desk, behind which Charles's chair was placed. Two walls of the room were lined with books from ceiling to floor. Against the third wall stood a glass-fronted display cabinet filled with a collection of glass, gold, and silverware. Past the desk Diana could see out the window onto The Mall and St. James's Park.

On the far side of the office was a long sofa with three comfortable chairs around it. The third room, just past the office, was the sitting room, about half again as large as the office. It was painted blue. Diana always felt surprise at the rather premeditated "clutter" of the sitting room. It was filled with literally hundreds of things he had collected from all over the world. There were also two more large bookcases, with books strewn all around the room, many of them on a table near the window. A television set and video cassette recorder stood in the far corner, alongside a truly magnificent stereo system.

In the center of the room a satin-covered sofa sat with chairs arranged around a glass-topped coffee table. The table was now set for supper with a white linen cloth over the glass, with silver cutlery, a bowl of fresh flowers, and one candlestick. Prince Charles stood up smiling at her, dressed formally in a dark suit.

Diana found herself once again in awe not only of this man but of the richly confortable, almost dated look of the environment around him—characteristic of inherited wealth. Of course, she was used to that; but with Prince Charles on hand, the reality of who he was became doubly underlined for her.

She sank down onto the sofa beside him, after he had

indicated that she should. A servant hung up her coat in a
closet and placed her bag next to her. Oddly enough, she
found herself trembling. Charles was talking. She had no
idea what he was talking about. In a way, the whole thing
seemed like a dream.

Now Diana realized something that surprised her. Prince
Charles was as nervous and as upset as she was. She had
never really known a man who could be so suave and cool at
all times. She had never seen him falter; even when he said
or did something wrong, he never lost his stride in correct-
ing it. But tonight he seemed shaken. His face was pale and
his eyes were shuttling back and forth in a most untharac-
teristic and sly manner.

He was talking about her trip to Australia. She tried to
indulge in intelligent conversation, but failed utterly. She
was jumpy, jittery. Now, for the first time in months, she
saw the tic at work on Prince Charles's cheek.

At a signal from him a servant glided into the room and
lit the candle. The flame flickered as dishes appeared, one
by one. Slowly they ate their food. Diana picked at her
food, actually not very hungry. She noticed that Charles
was not ravenous, either.

They finished the meal with a simple cheese and fruit,
much in the Spanish manner. Diana sat back and Charles
folded his arms.

"Your Australian visit comes at a very good time. It will
give you plenty of time to think."

"About what?" she asked.

"I thought that was obvious." Charles was puzzled.

"Nothing is obvious."

He smiled. "I want you to be my wife."

"Oh," she said faintly. "I had the feeling you did, but
you never said so."

"Not in so many words," Charles responded. "Will
you?"

Diana took a deep breath and opened her mouth to answer.

"I don't really expect an answer from you right now," Charles told her before she could speak. "It's a terribly important decision. I want you to think it over carefully."

Diana nodded. She was about to say something, when he went headlong into another discourse.

"I know that if you marry me, you'll have to give up your own comfortable lifestyle and become part of the royal family's life."

"Yes, Charles," she said. She could barely speak. Her heart was pounding. She had not realized the tremendous pressure she had been under. Now that he had asked her, there was a tremendous feeling of euphoria. She had told herself many times that she did not care what he decided; she knew now that she had *needed* this. She wanted to jump up and burst into song.

"You should have time to consider your future and what it will entail. I've thought it all out, and I think that you will be able to cope. But I don't know if you want to put yourself in a position of having to cope." He was smiling crookedly now, leaning forward, trying to lead her with his eyes.

"I see," she said. Why didn't he quiet down so she could answer him? It was a perfectly simple question.

"It's marvelous that your mother should provide a good time and a perfect place for self-assessment. I want you to relax there, take in the beach, sit in the sun, and think about us."

She waited. Was there any more? When he looked up at her, his eyes steady now, she leaned forward, her own eyes bright blue in the flickering candlelight, and said:

"Of course I'll marry you. What do you think I've been following you around all this time for?"

Charles seemed honestly surprised. Astonished would be

a more appropriate description. But then his face lighted up, and he leaned over and kissed her deeply.

For the next half hour they simply lolled in each other's happiness and began talking about their future, about their hopes, and started to make plans.

15

Diana Spencer drove back to Coleherne Court in a kind of golden haze. Her whole life had changed. She was intelligent enough to know that she would never be the same woman again. But it didn't matter. She had been in love with Prince Charles for a long time now; she had never wavered in her devotion.

"Get a good rest in Australia," Charles had told her just before she left. "I'll alert the right people. Naturally we can't let the news of the engagement leak out before the official announcement."

"When will that be?"

"Not until after you're back from Australia, love," Charles smiled. "Obviously."

"What date?"

"Let's try to make it sometime in March."

"Can we keep the press guessing that long?"

"We'll have to."

As she got out of her Mini Metro and hastened to the front door of her apartment, Diana suddenly realized that she would not even be living at Coleherne Court much longer. Charles had explained that she would have to move into Kensington Palace or maybe even Clarence House once she had become officially his intended. She now had an added problem. Should she tell her roommates now, or should she wait?

She let herself in the apartment, still trying to make up her mind. Actually, there was really no doubt in her mind from the beginning. Charles had cautioned her to be careful whom she told, and to keep the number limited: her mother, her stepmother, her father. Diana was simply not a person adept at deceit.

The moment she was inside, Carolyn glanced up and studied her curiously. "What's happened? You look different."

Diana closed the door and leaned back against it, almost as if she were posing for some motion picture scene.

"I'm engaged," she said simply.

Anne stared. "Officially?"

"To whom?" Virginia asked with a quick grin.

"I'm going to marry Prince Charles." Diana couldn't keep the big smile off her face. She drifted to the couch and sat down.

"He asked you?"

"Yes."

"What did he say? What did you do? Were you excited?"

"I can't answer you, really. I simply don't remember. It was all so wonderful. You've got to accept the fact that he asked me and that we're going to be married."

"When?"

"We don't know. Summer, I think." Diana realized she had made a mistake by revealing even that much. "You've got to promise. No one must know! It's got to be made official by an announcement from Buckingham Palace! Please! You've got to swear you won't tell!"

"We promise," they said.

Then Carolyn let out a little shriek of triumph, and ran over to Diana and threw her arms around her. So did Virginia, and then Anne. In a moment they were dancing crazily through the apartment, laughing and shouting at each other.

Diana collapsed in a chair, fanning her face to cool it off. She was flushed and breathing heavily.

Carolyn went into the kitchen, broke out a bottle of champagne, and poured four glasses. They all celebrated, toasting Diana and Charles. It got very late and they continued their party.

At the height of the celebration, the telephone rang. It was for Diana. Her father was on the line.

"I've just had the most extraordinary conversation with Prince Charles," he told her. "He called me 'sir,' and all that, and then he asked me for your hand! Said he wanted to marry you!"

Diana burst out laughing. "Yes! It's true!"

"I told him of course it was up to you. I said it was quite all right with me." There was a pause. "I wonder what he would have said if I had said 'no'?"

"Marvelous!"

"Of course, Raine and I knew you were in love a long time ago. But we didn't know about Charles."

"Daddy, I didn't either," Diana confessed.

"Well, he's a marvelous choice and I know you'll be very happy together."

"Thank you."

"Raine sends her best. She's dying to get on the telephone to her own mother."

"Mum's the word," said Diana. "Charles is adamant about that."

"Oh, quite. We understand. Only the closest family."

Diana's euphoria continued all the way through her flight to Australia. She left on Friday, flying first class to Sydney. She was not recognized at Heathrow and made the connection at Sydney for the flight to Canberra without being seen. A journalist at Sydney thought he recognized her but was not able to verify his sighting until he had wired London to confirm her presence in Australia. Confirmation was hard to come by.

Meanwhile, Diana disembarked at Canberra and was met by her mother and stepfather who drove her to Bloomfield, the sheep and cattle station owned by the Shand Kydds. Bloomfield was located near Yass, a settlement on the western slopes of the Great Dividing Range, about one hundred and fifty miles to the southwest of Sydney and twenty-five miles northwest of Canberra.

Diana was enchanted with the countryside. Bloomfield faced on the Murrumbidgee river, a westward-flowing river that finally met up with the Murray on its way to Adelaide, almost six hundred miles to the west.

Almost immediately Diana got into her work clothes and pitched in to help with the work. She had learned the rudiments in Scotland, and now ran her stepfather's tractor to help weed out the pastureland, overrun with Bathhurst burr, a messy growth that was the natural enemy of all Australian sheepmen.

Normally, Bloomfield was a quiet, remote spot, untouched by the urban excitement of Sydney. No one ever bothered to show up unless invited. Its very remoteness kept it inviolate. But now the Sydney reporter had received confirmation of a negative sort: Diana Spencer was apparently not in London.

A telephone call to Bloomfield ensued. "Good day," said a voice on the other end. "Is Lady Di there?"

Diana's stepfather immediately denied the fact that there

was anyone visiting the farm. "It's just me and two sick cows out in the yard. Would you care to come help me with them?"

"We hear she's at Yass."

"You've got the wrong continent," Shand Kydd said. "Try the Caribbean."

The press was not to be put off. Overnight remote Bloomfield became a kind of Sandringham down under, with journalists and photographers driving up to peer over the fences in the hope of sighting Diana Spencer.

"My daughter is not here," Diana's mother kept telling the more inquisitive ones. "You have got the wrong continent. She is in the sun somewhere, but not here."

By that time Diana was in touch with Charles by telephone. Charles immediately made contact with his good friends Lord and Lady Tryon—Kanga—who owned a cottage on Mollymook Beach on the east coast of Australia. Diana and her mother were immediately invited to spend their days there.

They drove down next day, Diana appearing on the beach shrouded only in headscarf and dark glasses, to sunbathe and picnic with the other vacationers. The subterfuge proved successful.

Now there was time to talk. Diana's mother was excited and happy about Charles's proposal, of course. So was Diana's stepfather. But her mother's happiness was tempered slightly by the realization of what her daughter's life was going to be in the future.

"I'm terribly happy for you, Diana, you know that. You know what you want, and you seem to have it all within your grasp. But in taking it, you'll be closing yourself off from some of the very finest and most private moments in your life."

"I've had my brushes with the press," Diana said. "It's not fun. But I think I can handle it."

"There's more than that," her mother went on. "You're really giving up your own freedom, your own individuality. Actually, you'll be second to the people of Great Britain."

"Mother, that's the way I want it."

"Yes. *I* can't say I would want it. When I marry a man, I want him completely to myself. I don't want to share him with the royal family and with the rest of the country."

Diana sensed that her mother was thinking beyond Diana and referring to Lady Fermoy, her mother, who had completely severed relations with her when she left Diana's father. There was a slight tone of malaise in her mother's voice when she mentioned the royal family.

"I'm just different from you," Diana said.

"I would hate it," Frances Shand Kydd burst out rashly. "I simply lack the ability to be polite and goody-goody twenty-four hours a day! And that's what you'll have to be when you're married and settled down."

"I love him, Mother."

"Of course you love him." She hesitated. "I don't know. It would seem to me that life with Prince Charles—and later on with the King of England—would be a sort of role in a West End play that went on forever."

"I suppose being a Princess is being an actress of sorts."

"And you won't have time to pursue your own commitments. I thought you wanted to teach."

"It's the children I love, not being a teacher. If I do have children—"

"I'm sure you'll have them. You're healthy and young." Her mother's blue eyes had a far-off look in them. "You'll be living in a goldfish bowl. You won't even be able to go down to the chemist's to get an aspirin."

Diana giggled. "Who ever heard of a Princess having a headache?"

"I suppose it will all turn out right. You'd better spend

the time while you're here enjoying your solitude. You're not going to be able to be alone again for the rest of your life."

Diana laughed off her mother's warnings. However, in the privacy of the beach, as she sat in the sun with her concealing dark glasses and headscarf on, she gazed out into the distance thinking about it. She considered herself lucky, really, that she had never become involved in a career interest of any kind. She would have become hooked on it; giving it up would have been much more difficult than consenting to become Charles's wife had been for her now.

She had always wondered why she had never taken up any professional or intellectual interest. Perhaps she was simply meant for one thing—the particular life she had now decided to make her own.

And yet . . .

Back at Bloomfield, the pressures were beginning to annoy Peter Shand Kydd. At the other end of the world there was also another person involved in petty annoyances.

Prince Charles tried to get through to speak to Diana. He did not know that the Shand Kydd cattle and sheep station had become tired of chasing off journalists and pretending that Diana was not there; they had installed a "watch" on the phone, using men from the staff to man the phones at the house, telling all callers that "Diana is not here."

"Who is this?" the Aussie operator asked when Charles's call came through.

"This is the Prince of Wales," Charles told him.

"Oh, sure," said the sheepman. "And I'm the Queen of the May."

"No, look, I really am," Charles protested, getting a bit hot. "I want to speak to Lady Diana Spencer."

"Sorry, mate," said the sheepman. "Nice try, but no cigar." And he hung up.

Charles had another private number to call, and he did so. This was a special line for Diana, installed for her use if she wanted to speak privately to anyone. Charles got through on that hot line and in a moment they were talking.

"I've got an idea," said Charles after telling her how much he missed her. "It's Andrew's birthday on February 19. Why don't you come home then?"

"But Charles! I was hoping to spend more time down here. The beach is just super!"

"Here's the point. The press will be thinking of Andrew on February 19. They'll be down at the Royal Naval Station at Culdrose in Cornwall, three hundred miles out of London. You see the picture. They won't be thinking of us at all. Isn't that the obvious time to come home?"

Diana could see the strategy. Again, it sounded exactly like Charles's military mind. Prince Andrew was a most attractive, good-looking, and photogenic person. He was developing into quite a dashing escort. Diana knew that he was called "Randy Andy" by most of the men and women she knew—and for good reason. Prince Andrew was always good for a couple of columns of hot copy.

Fleet Street would be decoyed away from London for Andrew's birthday. It would be the ideal time for her to come home and avoid the pressure of the paparazzi snapping pictures at her. And yet . . .

"We'll see," she told him. She hadn't intended it, but she sounded cross.

"I'll expect you on the nineteenth," he said as he hung up carefully.

"But, Charles—"

When she realized he had terminated the conversation, she slammed the phone down and bounced up in a fury. It was her last vacation; as her mother had pointed out, it was the last time she would be able to be alone with herself. Why was Charles trying to cut it short? He hadn't even listened to her objections to coming back on the nineteenth. Why couldn't he be reasonable?

Pacing up and down in the clean little room overlooking the white sounds of Mollymook Beach and the Pacific Ocean in the distance, she gazed out at the hot blue sky, the foaming waves, the sail boats in the distance, and the space and the tranquillity of Australia.

She picked up a magazine she had been flipping through and slammed it down. Her mood was ruined. She had been rested and feeling wonderful in the soft bracing air. She had been dreaming and free of all cares. Now she was back in the vicious cat-and-mouse game she had been playing with the royal family and the press. It wasn't *her* fault; she was caught in a crunch between the duty of the monarch and the love of the prince.

"What's the matter?" her mother asked, eyeing her curiously when she came down for tea.

"Charles wants me back February 19."

"But dear, that's cutting your vacation short!"

"I'm aware of that." She was abrupt.

"Can't you find out why? Perhaps—"

"It's an *order!* I have to go!" Her eyes were filling with tears.

"I see." Her mother eyed her shrewdly. "Well, then, I suppose you should go."

"I don't want to!" snapped Diana, pacing about angrily. "He can be so damned patronizing when he wants to be!"

"So can any man, Diana."

"Let's go to the beach. I don't want to talk about it."

She lay in the boiling sun soaking in the heat, her eyes closed, her thoughts drifting far off in some other world. The warmth of the day relaxed her and took the edge off her temper. After a while she sat up and put on her dark glasses once again to stare into the distance. There were tiny sailboats out there, moving back and forth in the breeze. She thought of the sea, and she thought of Charles because he loved the sea, too.

"It's the paparazzi," Diana said quietly.

Her mother frowned. "I don't quite understand what you're saying."

"You 'see, it's Prince Andrew's birthday. They'll be down trying to get pictures of him. He's marvelous copy. All those girl friends and pranks." She smiled.

Silence.

"If I fly in, perhaps there won't be anyone at Heathrow. And I can get home without being mobbed by the journalists."

"You certainly won't want to arrive home, all the way from the other side of the earth, frazzled and dazed by jet lag," her mother agreed, "with dozens of yammering journalists waving copy pads, microphones, and cameras in your face."

"If I can get a good night's sleep and unwind, then I can meet Charles for his morning workout with Allibar in Lambourn."

"I think it's a marvelous idea," said her mother. "Don't you agree?"

"Of course," she confessed, keeping her head down and hiding a smile.

"Then of course you're going on the nineteenth?"

Diana looked up, her face breaking in a big smile. She hugged her mother enthusiastically, and then began to sob in utter ecstasy.

"Thank you for not saying 'I told you so'!"

Her mother laughed. "But of course, I did tell you so."

"But nicely," Diana said, wiping her eyes with her handkerchief. "I'm going in the water." She rose quickly, tossed off her glasses and headscarf, and ran down over the sands into the blue Pacific Ocean.

Within minutes she felt invigorated, glowing, and ready

to take on the world again. When she ran back to sit by her mother, she was bubbling over with chatter. For an hour the two of them discussed the various phases of her training to be the Princess of Wales—training she would be undertaking at Clarence House under the tutelage of the Queen Mother and her own grandmother, Lady Fermoy.

When Charles called the next day, he was a bit hesitant. "Diana, if you don't really want to come home on the nineteenth—"

"Whatever gave you *that* idea, Charles?" She was cool and confident. "Honestly, you sometimes have no understanding of women!"

16

It was difficult for Diana to say goodbye to her mother and stepfather at the Canberra Airport, and it was even more difficult to say goodbye to Australia, where she had spent such a pleasant twelve days, but she managed it and boarded the Qantas flight for Heathrow, to arrive back in London on February 19.

Charles's paramilitary tactics had created the proper diversion and misdirection, and the Fleet Street gang was not in sight at Heathrow. Diana slipped easily through the crowds and got a cab into the city. In fact, she still needed a few things for the coming weekend, which she was to spend in Prince Charles's company, so she directed the cabby to Harrods, after leaving her bags at Coleherne Court.

She had put on a coat and tied a silk scarf over her head, looking exactly like one of the thousand-and-one other career girls living and working in the Knightsbridge area. She was pleased to see that no one took any notice of her.

Well, almost no one. A young woman did see her, but she was not a journalist; however, she had a good friend who was one. Unknown to Diana, her presence in London was known to Fleet Street almost within hours of her arrival there. However, no one was covering the apartment, and she was able to get into her car and drive out to Highgrove without anyone spotting her.

The house was almost completely refurbished and much of the furniture, assembled from various residences of the Queen, had been moved into the new mansion. An Irish couple who had been acting as custodians during the transition period between owners was still on hand. Charles had told Diana that he wanted her to see the new furnishings and request any changes she thought necessary.

Diana used M4, the big arterial superhighway that connected London with Bristol and the Cornwall area to the west and south. The trip to Highgrove, just north of M4, was a good hundred miles. She made it without incident. As she drove in through the iron gate and down the gravel driveway, she was watched by one of Charles's bodyguards and several local police stationed at the entrance.

Since the front of the house was visible from the roadway running alongside it, Charles was waiting inside for Diana to appear. When she opened the door and saw him, she let out a happy cry, and ran toward him. He had his arms opened wide to receive her. He enfolded her happily and kissed her.

She looked up into his face, her eyes sparkling. "I had a wonderful time, but I missed you!" she said.

He stroked her hair gently. "I missed you and *didn't* have a particularly wonderful time."

"Poor Charles!" she sighed.

They stood there enraptured for long moments, drinking in each other's presence. Finally Charles shook off his emo-

tion, and told her she should be looking over the rooms and
the furnishings. They had a great deal of work to do.

He led her through the huge house, room by room, and
they discussed each separate area as they surveyed it arm in
arm.

The guards and the Irish couple who prepared their dinner vanished afterward, and Diana sat with Charles in front
of the big log fire in the still unfinished, but mostly furnished, sitting room.

"It's finally here," Charles said after a long pause in the
cheerily warm room.

She turned to him, questioningly.

"The ring."

He removed a jewel case from his pocket and opened it.
She could see a sapphire glinting in the firelight, surrounded by fourteen perfect diamonds. She lifted the ring
out of its velvet case, holding it up to the light. The sapphire and diamonds sparkled and flashed in the shifting
firelight. She ran her finger lightly along the eighteen-carat
white gold in which the stones were set.

"May I?" he asked, taking the ring from her.

"Yes." She sank back in the divan, feeling his presence
and strength like an electrical force. He took her left hand
and gently slipped the ring on her finger. She stared down
at it, reluctant to let her eyes leave it.

"Oh, Charles!"

She reached up and kissed him fiercely, unable to re-
strain herself the way she knew she should. He held her
closely and finally let her go, sitting beside her with his arm
possessively around her shoulder.

"It's magnificent!"

"Now we're going to have to announce it, you know," he
said, smiling crookedly. "Anyone who sees that will know
what it means."

They sat up for awhile longer, making plans, but not setting a definite date for the announcement. Diana was still suffering from jet lag and Charles wanted to rest before his workout with Allibar in the morning, in preparation for a race at Chepstow Racecourse on Saturday.

Charles instructed his guard to waken him early. He then took Diana to one of the guest rooms, bid her goodnight, and vanished into the other part of the house to the bedroom he used when he was staying overnight.

Within minutes, Diana was sound asleep. She was so tired that she did not lie awake and think about her ring, or her fiancé, or her future. She slept like a baby. Too soon she was awakened by the sound of a knock on the door, and the movement of people in the house. She could smell coffee being made.

Quickly she got into her slacks and sweater, pulled on her boots, and was out in the kitchen. Charles was puttering around, getting his own things ready. Most of the gear was at the stables in Lambourn, about a fifty-mile drive to the east. Diana peered out the window. It was overcast and cold outside. She shivered, thinking how marvelous it had been on that beach in Australia on the other side of the world.

"Shall I take my car?" she asked Charles as they made away with their breakfast.

"I think we've fooled the press this time," he said with the ghost of a smile. "Why don't you come with me? No sense wasting all that petrol."

She giggled. Prince Charles sometimes acted the way some of his detractors said he acted: very tight with a pound.

Quickly they got into the blue Ford Granada and drove out through the gates onto the roadway, traveling south to M4, which they would use to travel east to Lambourn.

Behind them Diana could see a pair of security officers driving a Land Rover.

"I can see all those scribes now in Culdrose, covering Andrew's breakfast," Charles said with an amused smile.

"If I know Andrew," Diana said, "he'll probably be leading them a merry chase somewhere along Land's End."

"They'll know you're back in London Monday when you go back to work, but until then, we're on our own and clear of them. It'll be a marvelous weekend."

"In spite of the cold." Diana shivered. "It's not fair. Australia is warm and sunny—and we've got clouds and cold "

A Jaguar limousine edged around the driver's side past them. Diana happened to glance past Charles at the car and she let out a scream. "It's the press!"

Wild-eyed, Charles snapped his head to the right and found himself almost face to face with Arthur Edwards, a *Sun* photographer. Driving the car and sitting to the right of Edwards was Harry Arnold, a *Sun* reporter.

The two newsmen were as pop-eyed as were Diana and Charles. As she watched in horror—because she knew now that her weekend of privacy was definitely destroyed—she could see that Edwards was almost apoplectic with rage. Obviously, he did not have his camera within reach, or he would be taking pictures at that moment.

"Overconfidence has lost more battles than incompetence," Charles was muttering darkly. "We should have come out separately." He banged on the steering wheel in suppressed anger. "Just when we were about to have a few relaxing moments together!"

"Don't you see?" Diana said. "He'd be snapping pictures. I'll bet his camera is in the trunk of the car!"

Charles's expression relaxed. "You're right." He turned and watched them. The car was racing along beside the blue Ford Granada. "They're trying to figure out what to do."

"They'll have to drive off onto a lay-by, get out of the car, open the trunk and get his camera and equipment, and then come back," Diana said. "How much farther is it to Lambourn?"

"Only ten miles."

"Just keep going, Charles. I don't think they're going to get that picture after all."

Charles was musing as he studied them. "They must have left Cornwall at three in the morning. What would be the reason for that?"

Diana shook her head. "I don't know. Unless someone spotted me coming in yesterday."

"Of course! That's it. And they're trying to get back to London to cover you." Charles smiled. Later they found out that Charles's speculation was correct. When news of Diana's presence at Harrods had alerted Fleet Street, they had called their people back to the city for an early morning surveillance of Coleherne Court.

Just at that moment a car with flashing headlights came up on them from behind. Inside the Land Rover, the two Special Branch men were waving at the reporters in the Jaguar. But Arnold wasn't about to be outmaneuvered. He pushed his foot on the pedal, moving out ahead of the Ford Granada. Within minutes the Jaguar was almost out of sight.

Diana saw them on a lay-by, with Arnold out back frantically pulling the trunk open. Then, quite suddenly, the turn for Lambourn came up, and Charles drove off M4, made the turn, and headed for the lanes that led up to the stables.

He drove quickly into the private area where the stables were located. Without a word, Diana jumped out as he pulled over and crossed through the buildings to the edge of the riding field. She pulled her coat tighter against the chill of the morning and waited for Charles to appear on Allibar.

Charles was saddling up and soon came into sight. By now Diana could see the newsmen outside, unable to follow her into the field, which was private property, and not open to newsmen unless they were invited in. The two *Sun* reporters stood around chatting with Charles's security men; all of them were looking out over the race course in the field, waiting for Prince Charles to appear and take Allibar over the fences.

Dressed in racing gear and wearing the black crash helmet he wore when he jumped, he waved to them jauntily as he went by and started up the field where he would make his seven-mile canter around the jump circle.

Diana was watching him, waiting at the edge of the field close by where he would finish. The ride itself was uneventful. Diana waved at him, glad to see that he had not missed any of the hurdles. She always felt panicked when she watched someone else ride; she could not get out of her mind the pain and the fear she experienced at her own fall years ago.

Prince Charles reined up his mount within a few feet of her. His first run was over. He made a move to dismount. As he did so, Allibar jerked and twitched under him. Then the animal settled back, snorting strangely. Diana moved away from the horse's legs, surprised.

Aware that something was definitely wrong, Charles immediately jumped off and stood beside the big gelding, holding the reins.

"What's wrong?" Diana cried.

"I don't know. *Something.*"

Moments later, while the two of them were standing there motionless, the big horse twisted once again and fell to the ground with a shuddering crash. Horrified, Diana ran toward the horse in its agonies. She leaned over, holding the neck in her arms, trying to calm him.

Charles leaned over, took the horse from her, and patted him on the neck, trying to quiet him. But it was too late. Diana could see that the animal had stopped breathing. Allibar was dead.

She burst into tears. Charles, stunned and white-faced with shock, left the horse and put his arms around her to try to comfort her. She sobbed against his chest. Even though she did not ride, she loved Allibar as much as Charles did. He was holding her closely and smoothing down her hair as several of the stable boys jumped off their mounts and came over to help.

Diana and Charles walked away, both stricken by the sudden demise of Charles's favorite mount. A postmortem examination later determined that Allibar had died of a massive heart attack.

Tears were streaming down Diana's face as she followed Charles carefully over to his car. She managed to gain control over herself as she sat beside him. Finally she dried her eyes. She found that her makeup had been smeared by her tears; her face felt ruined. She knew she would be in for it when they finally met the reporters and photographers again. They would insist on pictures. She had been away for two weeks.

Charles was visibly upset. He sat behind the wheel, his face drawn and tense. He was sick with despair.

"We're going to Nick's," he told Diana.

She nodded. "I'll be all right."

"I'm going the back way. Let them try to follow us!"

He took the long way around, which kept the car out of sight of the waiting reporters, and soon arrived at the dead-end street in Lambourn where Nick Gaselee lived. Charles parked the car in front of the door, and Diana went inside with him. There were no reporters in sight.

They had breakfast with Nick and Judy Gaselee, who tried to console Charles over the loss of his horse. In the middle of their meal, there was a screeching of brakes, a slamming of car doors, and the sound of loud voices in the narrow street outside. Charles gritted his teeth.

"You'd think they would have a little more sensitivity," he muttered.

Gaselee turned to him. "I don't believe they know about Allibar."

Charles did not comment. Diana peeked out the window and saw a group of six men outside, standing in the bitter cold and stamping their feet to keep warm. They were smoking cigarettes and talking in groups—unusually loud, Diana thought.

She took a quick look in her pocket mirror and realized that she was in no shape to cope with the press. Her eyes were red and her makeup still smudged. Besides that, she felt absolutely awful. The sudden death of Allibar, combined with what was still an attack of jet lag, made her feel a hundred years old. Even the presence on her finger of her engagement ring could not cheer her up.

Noticing her peaked look, Charles went to the telephone. He called the special number that put him through to his backup Special Branch men in the car down at the end of the street. In a few minutes he came back.

"We're not going to let them photograph us together."

"But Charles—we've only one car this time."

He smiled grimly. "And they're not going to get a good shot of you alone, either."

Within minutes an ancient and battered Land Rover appeared at the door of the cottage. The photographers came out, the reporters moved over to it. Two security men elbowed their way through to the front door of the Gaselee cottage, carrying a folded horse blanket. Within minutes, Diana was covered by the horse blanket so that her upper body was not visible; the two security men huddled her between them, ducked her into the back seat of the Land Rover, and one of them sat there to cover her up.

Immediately, the other security man started the car and they sped off down the street. The paparazzi were once again balked.

A moment later Prince Charles sauntered out of the cottage and got into his blue Ford Granada. He was dutifully snapped by the photographers. The security men assigned to his car backed around in front of the reporters in the Jaguar, effectively blocking them off. Charles gunned the engine and sped out of the dead-end street with his own Special Branch men following.

The next day the writer of a story in the *Daily Mirror* said that it was "not the way to treat a lady," referring to the horse-blanket treatment, but it did quite effectively screen Diana's retreat. Once the two of them were at Highgrove, they chatted a moment together. Diana was too tired to go with him through the weekend, which had quite suddenly turned sour. Charles felt desolated by the death of Allibar; his special weekend was ruined, too.

Diana returned to Coleherne Court to rest. Charles drove north to Gloucestershire to hunt with The Beaufort.

The Fleet Street group was stunned to learn later in the day of the death of Allibar. One wrote a special note of apology to Prince Charles; he responded with a handsome reply in his own handwriting.

Later that same day, while Diana was in bed, Charles met with the Queen and Prince Philip. Charles was preparing for a trip to New Zealand, Australia, and the United States. He knew that if he waited too long to announce his

28 211

engagement, it would seem that he was putting on a disappearing act.

After the cat-and-mouse game Charles and Diana had been playing with the press, it was obvious that things were coming to a head. The announcement must be made as soon as possible. The date selected was four days from then—Tuesday, February 24, at 11:00 A.M.

Now word went out to the select few who had a right to know: Margaret Thatcher, the Prime Minister, and her staff at 10 Downing Street and other top cabinet ministers; the Archbishop of Canterbury, Dr. Robert Runcie; and the heads of the British Commonwealth all over the world.

Fleet Street knew *something* was up. On Monday calls came in to Buckingham Palace press officials; no one would confirm anything. At five o'clock, Lady Diana Spencer drove her car to Buckingham Palace. A free-lance photographer standing at the gate snapped her picture, and made a modest fortune with the prints.

Later that night, Diana was formally introduced to Chief Inspector Paul Officer, who would act as her bodyguard from that moment on. Officer had served Prince Charles for twelve years. Then Diana packed her bags and moved into a bedroom at Clarence House, the London home of the Queen Mother. The mansion is located some five hundred yards from Buckingham Palace off St. James's Street in Piccadilly.

The first thing in the morning, she took Prince Charles's blue estate car and drove to her hairdresser's, Kevin Shanley, in South Kensington. Shanley did her sisters' hair, too.

As she went into Shanley's establishment she waved her left hand at Shanley and his assistants.

"What do you think of that?"

Shanley stared at the huge diamond-and-sapphire engagement ring.

"Well, Lady Diana, all the best," Shanley said. The rest of his crew simply stood there staring at the ring, making appropriate sounds of approval.

Then they set to work on Diana's thick blond hair, washing it and setting it. When they were through, Diana got into the car and Officer drove her over to Buckingham Palace.

Meanwhile, there was a news leak; there was *always* a leak. The morning's *London Times* scooped Fleet Street and the world, promising that this would be the day. And, at 11:00 A.M., the *Times* was proved right. The word went out from Buckingham Palace:

> "It is with the greatest pleasure that the Queen and the Duke of Edinburgh announce the betrothal of their beloved son, the Prince of Wales, to the Lady Diana Spencer, daughter of the Earl Spencer and the Honourable Mrs. Shand Kydd."

17

Within the few moments it took for the announcement of her engagement to Prince Charles to be made, Lady Diana Spencer's life changed forever. She had anticipated that there would be a difference between plain Lady Diana Spencer, private citizen, and Lady Diana Spencer, fiancée of the Prince of Wales—but she had never realized the full scope of the difference.

The hours that followed flowed by like a speeded-up motion picture film. She could only look back on it later and marvel at its infinite variety. There were interviews, statements, the press, the public—and at all times she could feel the urgency to appear calm and cool on the surface in spite of the churning excitement that possessed her.

Most challenging of all was the five-minute television dialogue she and Charles held with two hard-nosed reporters—a brief interview finally uniting both the Prince of Wales and Lady Diana Spencer in front of the cameras for the world to see.

Diana relaxed during the first few moments of the dialogue—she let Charles carry the burden of the questions. He told the two interviewers that he was absolutely delighted at the engagement.

"I was surprised that Diana agreed to take me on," he admitted with a smile.

After some more throwaway comments, one of the interviewers turned to Diana and asked how she felt.

"Absolutely thrilled." She glanced at him. "With Prince Charles near me, nothing can go wrong."

"Do you love the Prince?"

"Of course!" Diana burst out with a bright smile.

They were asked where they had met. Diana picked it right up and said they had first met in November 1977. She said Prince Charles came as a friend of her sister Sarah for a shoot and that she never saw Prince Charles before that time. Of course, that wasn't quite true, but it did make the right point. "I was paired with Prince Andrew." She giggled. "Which really wasn't too bad, after all."

Almost instantly she realized that she was reverting to adolescent giggles again. And yet she could sense that her interviewers and all the television crew around her were watching with unrestrained admiration.

"When did the engagement take place?"

"Almost three weeks ago, believe it or not, before Diana went to Australia." Charles went on to say that he decided he would ask her then to let her have a chance to think it over and either accept or turn him down when she got back. "But, to my amazement and utter delight, she accepted," he said with a dazed smile.

As for the date of the wedding, Charles said they hadn't yet decided. He then told them that they planned to live down in Highgrove in Gloucestershire, and also have an apartment in London.

Diana was asked if she liked being in the public eye. She responded that it was quite daunting, but hoped it wouldn't be too difficult.

"Did your age difference ever bother you?"

Diana quickly answered that she never really thought about it.

Charles was slower. "It's only a twelve-year difference. Lots of people have got married with that sort of age difference. I always feel you are as old as you think or feel you are. I think Diana will keep me young. That's a very good thing. I shall be exhausted."

And there were interviews with the press, too. Diana remembered one exchange of conversation with the reporter who had first introduced her to the world six months before in Scotland—James Whitaker.

"Why has such a fuss been made of me?" she asked him, feeling that she might at last get some kind of honest answer about the pressure of the past months. "Do you and your colleagues think that I am the right person for him just because I don't have a past? Is it only really because I don't have a record of jumping in and out of bed with boy friends? What makes me so different?"

Whitaker smiled. "There are many, many reasons why so many people want you to marry him," he told her.

"What is one of them?"

Whitaker pondered. "If you were to walk into a room in which you were alone with the Queen, the Duke of Edinburgh and the Prince of Wales, would that make you a little nervous?"

"No," Diana told him. "Why should it?"

Whitaker smiled at her. "Isn't that enough?"

Diana didn't understand.

"Being with Prince Charles changes most people, makes them nervous, unreal. There are very few people who don't change when they're with him. You are one of them. Don't ever lose it."

Later in the afternoon, Diana was driven back to Cole-herne Court by Paul Officer to pick up the rest of her things. She would be living at Clarence House for some time. As she entered her apartment, she saw two Special Branch guards on duty there. Officer told her that they had been there since the time of the engagement announcement.

Her three good friends were there, waiting. They had heard the announcement and congratulated her again. Diana went to her room and collected everything she had not yet packed up. She had never been the neatest person with her possessions, but now she left the room clean and tidy. She sat there for a moment, tears of happiness and some of regret welling in her eyes.

She was just a bit weepy when she came out to say goodbye to Carolyn Pride, Virginia Pitman and Anne Bolton.

"For God's sake, ring me up," she begged. "I'm going to need you!"

As her guard led her out of the apartment, the usual group of reporters tripled or quadrupled. Everyone seemed to be there. Flashbulbs popped, reporters yelled questions—it was pandemonium. Officer pushed through the mob and got her into the Prince of Wales's blue Ford Granada and she sank back in the seat, gripping her shoulder bag and trying to look cool and collected.

The drive to Clarence House—really only a hop, skip, and a jump—took a great deal of maneuvering, with the press in hot pursuit. Finally, when she got out of the car and mounted the steps of Clarence House, she turned half-way up the steps, paused, smiled radiantly, and waved her hand at the press in a kind of "already regal" manner, as one scribe put it.

Clarence House was almost like coming home for Diana.

The next morning she sat down to breakfast with the Queen Mother, whom she had known intimately all her life, and with her own grandmother, Lady Fermoy, who had acted as her mother during her father's divorce proceedings.

Diana dressed in jeans and a sweater; although there were eyebrows lifted in the staff at Clarence House, no one said anything aloud. The current casual fashion of dress had apparently been more or less accepted there.

For the next four days Diana lived at Clarence House. She was more or less in school again. The Queen Mother was giving her the essentials of public service, trying to prepare her for a life in society on a truly royal level.

Diana learned that she could never walk beside Prince Charles; he would always precede her. She learned that she could never call him by his Christian name in public anymore. He would be Your Royal Highness. She learned that she would always be the highest-ranked woman in the room with the exception of the Queen and the Queen Mother.

She learned the wave that would be her special gesture for her lifetime—from the elbow, with the wrist frozen. She learned the smile, that pleasant smile that must be long and hard, with a certain warmth, and never allow it to disintegrate into a leer.

And she had lessons in wardrobe. She must choose dresses that would make her stand out. She must choose her shoes with low heels so she would never tower over her husband. She must choose hats that did not hide her face. She must learn to look exclusive without appearing too extravagant.

For the wedding, she practiced the art of walking with a train. She wrapped a heavy curtain around her waist and strode up and down the rooms.

But those details were minor ones. Actually, there wasn't much she needed to learn. The Queen Mother and Lady

Fermoy had inculcated a great deal of the art in her during her youth.

After four days of intensive training at Clarence House, Diana moved out to stay with her sister, Lady Jane Fellowes, at Kensington Palace. And there she planned to stay until the wedding. The details of the coming ceremony took up most of her time. Discussions with Charles were long and detailed.

"I want this to be a musical wedding," Charles told her. "The acoustics at Westminster Abbey aren't all that good. I'd like St. Paul's."

Diana had discussed the wedding site with her mother in Australia. "There are reasons even I might not like Westminster Abbey," her mother had said. "I was married there, you know. It would be extremely painful for me to see you married there."

She mentioned this to Charles. "Would it be a bad sign for us to start out our marriage there, in view of what happened in my family?"

Charles agreed that it would be unfortunate. "I have sad memories of Westminster Abbey, too—no fault of the Abbey. That's where my great uncle's funeral was held."

"As it happens," Diana confided with a smile, "St. Paul's Cathedral was designed by my fourth cousin, nine times removed—Sir Christopher Wren."

Even Charles was startled at that revelation.

"Oh, I'm related to almost everyone in England!" Diana laughed.

There were arguments for Westminster Abbey, of course. All the weddings of the century had been held there: the Queen's, the Queen Mother's, Princess Anne's, Princess Margaret's, and Princess Alexandra's.

In the end they decided on St. Paul's.

"I won't have a cold wedding day," Charles had told

Diana many times. The date for the ceremony was finally set for July 29, 1981.

Diana, Charles, the Queen, and the Lord Chamberlain—Lord Maclean—met to discuss the ceremony. It was the Lord Chamberlain's duty to carry out the plans once they were formulated.

The question of money soon came up. It would be more expensive holding the wedding at St. Paul's, but the difference was not what bothered the Lord Chamberlain the most. "Think again," he advised them, "if, for no other reason, than that we are worried that we will not have enough soldiers to line the route properly."

Charles screwed up his forehead in a quizzical frown. "Well, simply stand them further apart."

Within the week Diana's mother flew in from Australia. They met privately at Kensington Palace with Lady Jane, and mother and daughter let their hair down and talked about the final details of the wedding.

Charles was scheduled to make a five-week tour of New Zealand, Australia, Venezuela, and the United States in late March. Between February 24 and March 24, Charles and Diana would make their first public appearance together as an engaged couple. Except for the one series of pictures the press had taken when their engagement was announced, there had been no other pictures of them together.

Diana planned her premiere appearance in public with Prince Charles with the precision of an armed-forces engagement with the enemy. Charles had already intended to take her out on March 9 to the Royal Opera House Development Appeal; the site of the opera was Goldsmith's Hall in London.

For the occasion, Diana chose a pair of modern clothes designers from whom she had bought dresses for some time now. David and Elizabeth Emanuel would create a formal gown for her. They had been in business on exclusive Brook Street, London, in a posh section of Mayfair, for only four years. But during that time they had done very well for themselves, attracting bluebloods and entertainment personalities alike. Jane Seymour, the actress; Bianca Jagger, Mick Jagger's wife; and Alana Stewart, Rod Stewart's wife—all were their clients. So were Princess Anne, and Princess Michael of Kent, the Queen's first cousin.

It was to David and Elizabeth that Diana finally turned almost in desperation after she had scoured Beauchamp Place without finding what she wanted—a smart, sharp, ball gown for her evening's appearance.

She told the Emanuels that she would be making her public debut on March 9. "I need something smashing to wear."

"Would you be a little more specific?" David asked.

Diana glanced around the shop, her eyes alert and searching. Hanging on a rail she spotted the shell of a low-cut black strapless creation that was in the planning stage.

"That," she cried happily. "Can you make *that* up?"

"In a few days," David promised.

And so That Dress was born—the low-cut, strapless, unforgettable gown Lady Diana Spencer wore to Goldsmith's Hall on her debut as Princess-to-be.

When some days later Diana got into the gown she was absolutely bowled over. The bra-less, black silk-taffeta evening gown and full skirt did everything for her that she had wished for. It buried forever the impression that she was shy, maidenly, and naive.

Although brand new in design, it was modeled on the concept of a much earlier era in England—that of Nell Gwynn, the notorious mistress of the lusty monarch Charles II. Its motif was a combination of sex, glamour, and youth; the gown was low-cut and revealing. Designed with broad shoulder straps, the bodice was dotted with black sequins and held up by Diana's figure and nothing else. The gown was topped off with a matching black cape. It would have inspired wolf whistles even in Nell Gwynn's time.

"It's exquisite," Diana told them, turning around and viewing herself in the full mirror. She had been annoyed from the first at the press for dubbing her "Shy Di" because of her blushes and her youth. This, she knew, would show them who she really was.

Even Charles's jaded eyes popped when he drove by to pick her up at Kensington Palace in his official limousine. The press was out in full force at Goldsmith's Hall. Diana and Charles exchanged small talk in the car and Diana was pleased to see her fiancé's amused anticipation of the unveiling of his future wife.

They pulled up in front of the hall. Charles emerged first to help her out. The paparazzi were standing around waiting, with flashbulbs and cameras and television equipment poised. Diana heard Charles's somewhat proud voice:

"Wait till you get an eyeful of this!"

Then it was Diana's turn. Charles took her hand and she climbed out of the limousine into the full glare of the public eye. Britain's Independent Television News was positioned directly above and in front of her. As she straightened up in front of the cameras with Charles holding her arm she smiled dazzlingly at everyone. She could hear gasps from the crowd of onlookers. Some of the journalists were even giving low whistles. Conscious and proud of her shoulders and low-cut bodice, Diana straightened and walked toward the corridor with her fiancé.

In the twinkling of an eye—or, more accurately, in the pop of a flashbulb—Lady Diana Spencer knew that she had created an image for herself that would not soon be forgotten in Great Britain or in the world. From the moment she left the limousine until she was seated, photographers were popping bulbs at her and snapping pictures. The television cameras held her in their lenses as long as possible. Commentators gave low-voiced descriptions that were unneeded with the excitement of her visual presence.

Diana could feel that Charles was sharing in her glorious debut, amused and at the same time very proud. She could sense it in his expression and in the tension of his hand. There was an electricity in the air and Diana knew that she was the cause of it. She had never before been able to project such a positive image. She felt like a star; and she *was* a star.

The concert was excellent, but Diana was the focus of all attention. Even afterwards, at a buffet supper held to honor the Royal Opera House Development Fund, Diana was still the center of attention. But Diana was still very much herself.

A woman seated next to her at the buffet saw her gently rubbing her side, and asked if she had a sore back.

Diana smiled. "Not at all. It's just that I've got pins and needles in my bottom from sitting still so long. I've never had pins and needles in my bottom before in my life!"

Diana would never be stuffy.

Not all the Commonwealth approved of Diana's revealing costume. She later learned that the switchboard at Buckingham Palace blazed like a lighthouse on a stormy night, with calls protesting the unseemly exposure of the Princess-to-be. Some callers even complained that the royal family was trying to take England back into the lawlessness and prurience of the Swinging Sixties—forgetting for the moment, or ignorant of history, that the era was actually the Restoration of 1660, not the 1960s.

The *Daily Mirror* headlined their picture of Diana's décolletage:

LADY DI TAKES THE PLUNGE

The *Sun* said:

DI THE DARING

It ran one picture of her on the front page, and three on an inside page. Columnist Jean Rook of the *Daily Express* discussed the dress, noting: "You can't have too much of as good a thing as Lady Diana." *Time* magazine mentioned her "sexpot role."

After Charles had delivered her back to Kensington Palace, Diana sank back in a chair and stretched her legs. She knew that she had finally established herself as a no-nonsense, natural, strong-minded young woman, firm enough in her own opinions on style and living to create an image for herself in the world. As a future Princess of Wales she would be every bit as much a personality in her own right as the Prince of Wales was in his.

The four months between Diana's "debut" and the wedding were busy ones. Much of that time would be lonely for Diana. Prince Charles was about to leave for his visit down under.

Meanwhile, he had replaced Allibar with a brown gelding named Good Prospect, which proved to be a far more active mount than Allibar. In two successive races Charles was thrown during the month of March.

The first fall occurred on March 13, a definitely bad-luck Friday the thirteenth, at Sandown Park. Charles ended up with a bloody nose, nothing more serious. Diana was a bit shaken by the fall, but Judy Gaselee took care of her and helped steer her away from the crush of reporters and the public.

Four days later Charles was racing at Cheltenham, and Good Prospect again threw him. Diana was in the stands watching and suffering. Somehow she got through the second fall; there was a great deal of sympathy from the public for her.

A week and a half later, Charles left for New Zealand. Diana was coping as well as she could with all the details of royal procedure and protocol, but she needed Charles's common sense and his puckish humor to get through the morass of instructions and briefings.

"Life in Buckingham Palace isn't too bad," she wrote to a close friend. "But too many formal dinners (yuk!)."

She accompanied Charles to Heathrow on March 29 to see him off. The press was there, reporters surging in on her. As Charles strode off to board the plane, to her unspeakable horror, Diana suddenly burst into tears.

She was furious with herself. The press was enchanted. Diana fled to Kensington Palace and kept out of sight for twenty-four hours.

"It's bad enough to be in love," she told her sister Jane. "It is simply too much to let it all show to everybody out there. They don't really care about me at all—just the role I'm playing!"

Diana had instructed David and Elizabeth to design her wedding dress, and when she visited them, she found them becoming as paranoid about the press as she had become.

"We keep the shades drawn," Elizabeth confessed to Diana. "I've heard that people with telescopes can peer through windows."

One thing the Emanuels were worried about was the fact that Diana was losing weight. She had always been a bit plump, but certainly not too fat. She was now ten pounds lighter than she had been when the announcement was made. The problem for the Emanuels was a very real one; what if she didn't fit into her wedding dress?

On May 3 Charles flew back to Scotland to meet Diana

privately at Balmoral Castle. It was a welcome respite, but Diana found the time passing much too rapidly. After several days of seclusion they were back in the swim of it.

The Saturday before the wedding, the tension was beginning to tell on Diana. What didn't help at all was Charles's determination to continue his polo appearances. After those two falls from Good Prospect, Diana had really had enough. The accidents had reinforced her own reservations about riding.

Photographers and journalists kept closing in on her all through the match. Finally, Diana could stand it no more. She suddenly burst into tears, and had to leave in the middle of the match.

Next day, however, she was back, determined and sedate. She even talked to the press. One of her main functions in life after the wedding Wednesday, she said, would be to be a good wife.

"Life will obviously be much busier," she said. She said she hoped that she and Prince Charles would have an opportunity to have some time to themselves. She seemed to be eyeing the press as she made that point.

"It has taken a bit of getting used to the cameras," she noted. "But it is wonderful to see people's enthusiastic reaction. It is most rewarding and gives me a tremendous boost. I have been extremely touched by everyone's enthusiasm and affection. And the Prince of Wales has made everything far easier for me."

One of the women reporters said that she thought Diana had lost about fifteen pounds during the past few months, thus hinting that life as the Princess-to-be might be leaving something to be desired. Diana did not comment.

Charles helped the England II team defeat Spain on the field that day for the Silver Jubilee Cup. He made the eighth goal that helped England win, 10–5, over Spain.

On the eve of the wedding, Diana and Charles did not see one another—exactly as tradition required. Somehow Diana felt that she had not really seen enough of him after their engagement was announced. She moved back to Clarence House and slept there, retiring early for a good rest.

18

Wednesday, July 29, 1981, dawned overcast and gray. Lady Diana Spencer awoke refreshed and happy at 6:00 A.M. She had let Prince Charles attend the fireworks display alone and light the first of the one hundred and one beacons which would carry the inaugural message to all corners of the British Isles. The chain stretched as far south as the Channel Islands and as far north as the Shetlands, and from Northern Ireland, Land's End and Caernarvon in the west of East Anglia and the Isle of Thanet in the east.

This was the bridegroom's symbolic act of announcing the wedding. Afterward, there were fireworks and music as choirs burst into song. Finally, a giant catherine wheel, forty feet across, shot flames out to over a hundred feet.

Soon after she arose, Diana began her preparations for the wedding, thinking that she must be like some princess from medieval days, surrounded by attendants and helpers. Her hairdresser, Kevin Shanley, was one of the first to appear on the job. She warned him to do her hair in a light and simple coiffure; she was to wear a tiara.

The tiara, an ornate but unobtrusive affair, was a Spencer family heirloom, incorporating an intricate en-twined-star-and-flower design with a heart-shaped cen-terpiece. She was going to wear a pair of earrings, but that was the only jewelry.

Barbara Daly was doing her makeup; she worked on Diana very carefully, having little to do. "Lady Diana blushes very prettily," she told onlookers. She did not need to add much to her fair and fresh complexion. Diana could hear the sounds of the crowd assembling at The Mall not far from Clarence House as her attendants worked on her.

Clive Shilton of Covent Garden was present to select her shoes.

Luckily, Diana's loss of weight had been compensated for by the Emanuels. The gown fitted perfectly. It was made of ivory-colored pure silk taffeta and old lace, and embroidered with tiny mother-of-pearl sequins and pearls. It had a lace flounce around the neck. The full skirt was worn over a crinoline, with a sweeping train twenty-five feet long, trimmed with embroidered lace.

For her "something old," Diana had chosen an antique lace stitched around the neckline of her gown. For her "something borrowed," the Spencer family tiara. For her "something blue," a blue bow sewn into the waistband of her gown, along with a tiny gold horseshoe for luck.

By 9:00 A.M., the overcast had disappeared, the sky out-side was blue, and there was only a tiny patchwork of cloud. The air was warming up.

Now came Diana's wedding bouquet. It was made up of British-grown flowers: a center of gardenias held up by golden Mountbatten roses (to honor the memory of Lord Mountbatten), surrounded by lily of the valley and white freesia, with a cascade of white odontoglossum orchids and stephanotis. Also included was a sprig of veronica from the bush on the Isle of Wight which had been grown from Queen Victoria's wedding bouquet.

By 10:00 A.M., most of the party had assembled at Buckingham Palace to depart for St. Paul's Cathedral. Those first to leave the Palace were the crowned heads of Europe, including King Olav of Norway, Queen Margrethe of Denmark, King Gustaf of Sweden, Queen Beatrix of the Netherlands, Grand Duke Jean of Luxembourg, King Baudouin of Belgium, Prince Franz Josef of Liechtenstein, and Princess Grace of Monaco.

Next, the five bridesmaids and two pages left with Lady Sarah Armstrong-Jones, Charles's cousin, at their head. They included Miss India Hicks, Miss Catherine Cameron, Miss Sarah Jane Gaselee, and Miss Clementine Hambro; the two pages were Lord Nicholas Windsor and Mr. Edward van Cutsem. These guests were driven off in limousines.

The Queen's horse-drawn carriage left the Palace at 10:22 A.M. In an open semilandau, drawn by four handsome grays, the Queen was accompanied by the Duke of Edinburgh in the full-dress uniform of Admiral of the Fleet. The Queen's group of eight carriages was followed by the bridegroom's procession. Charles was dressed in a specially tailored Royal Navy "Number One" uniform; his brother, Prince Andrew, at his side, was in full dress uniform. They sat in a State Postillion Landau, built in 1902 for Edward VII.

Diana found her father waiting for her downstairs in the courtyard of Clarence House, standing next to the Glass Coach in which they would be driven to the cathedral. They climbed in together, sitting in the narrow back seat. This was the only closed coach of the horse-drawn carriages. It was originally purchased by George V for his coronation seventy-one years earlier. Diana had a light veil on, one through which the crowds could see her face.

At about 10:35 A.M., the Glass Coach made its first jolting movements from the yard of Clarence House and turned down into The Mall. Diana could see out through the veil, but felt hemmed in by the immense amount of tulle that made up the length of her train. She and her father looked out at the crowded area around The Mall.

She could see the balcony of Buckingham Palace to her right, sporting its famous crimson drapes. Lining The Mall were one hundred-fifty gold-crowned and tasseled flagstaffs, each bearing an enormous Union Flag. Beyond that, the lush green of the foliage stood in its lovely summer leaf. Every intervening lamp post was decorated with a basket of delicate summer flowers—verbenas, petunias, phlox—a profusion of royal purple and blue.

As the Glass Coach made its jarring way down through The Mall, Diana looked out at the flagstaff of St. James's Park; each was surrounded by three spiked poles draped with Union Jacks, and supporting a platter of fresh yellow, white, and cream flowers. They passed through the Admiralty Arch, past Trafalgar Square, and into the Strand; there an array of red, white, and blue banners were linked with bunting and backed by huge pictures.

Past the Strand the carriage jolted up Fleet Street, past all the offices of the big newspapers, up Ludgate Hill to St. Paul's Cathedral. As the Glass Coach drew up in front of the church, the crowds broke into loud cheers. Diana's father climbed down and helped her out to the street level, the bridesmaids gathered about to help her with her train.

Diana glanced around at the crowd and turned to her father. "Is he here yet?" she asked mischievously.

They climbed the steps and entered the cathedral. Jeremiah Clarke's *Trumpet Voluntary* blared out as the two of them walked down the aisle. Twenty-five hundred guests were waiting and watching in the cathedral as she traversed the six hundred-fifty feet of red-carpeted aisle to the dais of the church. It took her three-and-a-half minutes.

She and her father joined Charles and Prince Andrew. Diana stood beside Charles. She turned to him. He glanced at her warmly and lovingly. Quickly she clutched his hand and he squeezed back. The Queen, who was watching closely, smiled benignly.

The choir began singing Purcell's hymn, *Christ is made the sure foundation*.

As the hymn ended, there was an enormously significant silence throughout the cavernous cathedral. The Dean of St. Paul's, the Very Reverend Alan Webster, came forward to introduce the service.

"Dearly beloved, we are gathered here . . ." He concluded with the traditional challenge: "If any man can show just cause, why they may not lawfully be joined together, let him now speak, or else hereafter forever hold his peace."

No word was spoken.

Diana saw Charles flick away a sudden tear that had unexpectedly appeared in his eye. Diana smiled to herself; she knew Charles well enough now to realize that underneath, he was as sentimental as she. No one could guess it to watch him, but she knew better.

The Archbishop of Canterbury, the Most Reverend Robert Runcie, wearing an impressive new silver-gray cape and miter, now approached to preside over the wedding vows. He asked the bridegroom and bride, in turn, whether they were prepared to love, comfort, honor, and keep one another in sickness and health.

The 1928 version of the 1662 prayer was used in this exchange; Diana had chosen to omit the promise to obey, in full accordance with Charles. Originally the pledge had been inserted in the marriage vows during the Middle

Ages. Not only was the bride expected to obey, but to be "bonny and buxom in bed and board."

Diana could remember with amusement the reaction of the Archbishop when they had told him to drop the traditional "obey" from the ceremony. He had agreed: "It's a bad thing to start your marriage off with a downright lie."

Now the Archbishop was asking her to repeat after him the names of Prince Charles. Momentarily forgetting herself, she agreed to take "Philip Charles Arthur George" to be her wedded husband, rather than "Charles Philip Arthur George," the man who was standing at her side. Almost immediately after that, Charles fluffed the line "and all my worldly goods with thee I share," saying, "and all thy goods with thee I share."

After the promises, Charles placed the ring handed to him by Prince Andrew on Diana's finger, declaring in a firm voice: "With this ring I thee wed." With the pronouncement, "I now pronounce you man and wife," there was a roar of applause from the crowd outside the cathedral; the sound was a sudden reminder that not only the twenty-five hundred in the cathedral were listening to every word being said, but much of the world outside as well.

Lady Diana was Lady Diana no longer. She was now Princess of Wales, Countess of Chester, Duchess of Cornwall, Duchess of Rothesay, and so on—the third lady in the land after the Queen and the Queen Mother.

Now William Mathias' shrill and triumphant arrangement of Psalm 67, *Let the people praise Thee, O God*, sounded. Intoning the words of the hymn was George Thomas, Speaker of the House of Commons and personal friend of Prince Charles. "Though I speak with the tongues of angels and have not love . . ."

The Archbishop began his address.

> Here is the stuff of which fairy tales are made:
> the prince and princess on their wedding day. But
> fairy tales usually end at this point with the sim-
> ple phrase, "They lived happily ever after." This
> may be because fairy tales regard marriage as an
> anticlimax after the romance of courtship.
> This is not the Christian view. Our faith sees
> the wedding day not as the place of arrival, but
> the place where the adventure really begins.
> There is an ancient Christian tradition that
> every bride and groom on their wedding day are
> regarded as a royal couple.

The Archbishop then went on to describe various elements
of weddings.

> Those who are married live happily ever after
> the wedding day if they persevere in the real ad-
> venture which is the royal task of creating each
> other and creating a more loving world.
> That is true of every man and woman undertak-
> ing marriage. It must be specially true of this mar-
> riage in which are placed so many hopes.

He concluded:

> This is our prayer for Charles and Diana. May the
> burdens we lay on them be matched by the love
> with which we support them in the years to come.
> However long they live, may they always know
> that when they pledged themselves to each other
> before the altar of God, they were surrounded

and supported, not by mere spectators, but by the sincere affection and active prayer of millions of friends. Thanks be to God.

The choir sang Parry's powerful anthem, *I was glad*, the words of which, taken from Psalm 122, incorporated the prayer, "Peace be within thy walls and plenteousness within thy Palaces."

Diana and Charles knelt at the High Altar, a stark, gold-ornamented fixture in Sicilian marble amid the rich browns, golds, and reds on all sides. Now the Lesser Litany was intoned and sung. Prayers followed, uttered by the non-Anglican Cardinal Basil Hume, Roman Catholic Archbishop of Westminster, and the Right Reverend Andrew Doig, Moderator of the Church of Scotland and a member of the Anglican Community of the Resurrection.

Cecil Spring Rice's poem of dedication and spiritual allegory followed: "I Vow to Thee, My Country," sung to Gustav Holst's serene and imposing music. The Archbishop gave his final blessing. As the "Amens" faded away, the south transept erupted with a drumroll and fanfare heralding Sir David Willcocks' soaring arrangement of the national anthem.

The clergy moved from the sanctuary to the Dean's Aisle to the right. Diana and Charles followed, with their families bringing up the rear. There they signed the two registers—a church register for the parish record, and a royal register. Signing were Prince Charles, writing his name for the first time, "Charles P.," and Lady Diana, signing for the last time, "Diana Spencer." The Queen and Prince Philip, the Queen Mother, Prince Andrew, Princess Anne and Lady Sarah Armstrong-Jones followed.

During the signing, New Zealand Maori soprano Kiri Te Kanawa, a favorite of Charles's, sang Handel's aria "Let the bright Seraphim." The chorus followed with "Let their celestial concerts," from *Samson*.

As the Queen stepped forward to sign the register as witness, Prince Charles bowed to her, and Diana, now the new Princess, dropped a deep curtsy to her. The newlyweds began their walk down the red carpet. Diana drew back her veil; she blushed and smiled. She turned to her husband—he was tall, slim, serious, regal. He linked his arm warmly with hers.

Sir Edward Elgar's "Pomp and Circumstance March No. 4" resounded loudly through the cathedral. They proceeded down the red carpet to the west door. Outside the sunshine was blinding. The crowd was cheering. There were thousands of faces, flags, and cries. Now, as Diana and Charles came out into the street, there was pandemonium—cheers, shouts, bells, rattles, and whistles and hooters. Diana smiled broadly and waved back to the crowd; another cheer resounded, shaking the air.

She hurried down the steps with her husband to the waiting landau, as the Queen and the royal family clustered around the cathedral door to watch their departure. The trip back to Buckingham Palace was simply a moment of relaxation for the two of them. The street erupted in a frenzy of jubilation as the carriage jolted back to Buckingham Palace. A silver horseshoe gleamed in the landau, and a shower of rice, confetti, and rose petals rained down on them from upper windows all along the processional route.

By the time the carriage neared the palace, the procession had slowed to a walking pace so that the screaming, milling mass of well-wishers could get a better look at the two of them. Diana sank back in the cushions, waving and beaming. Charles seemed stunned by all the heartfelt acclaim. The two of them giggled and continued waving. The sun shone on them warmly and the air had brightened to a perfect day.

The crowd surged around Buckingham Palace, waiting. At 1:15 P.M., Diana and Charles, with the royal family surrounding them, came out onto the balcony above the crowd. A tumultuous roar greeted them. They waved to the crowds and to the television cameras recording it all for the world and for posterity.

They retired to start their wedding breakfast, but the crowd would not let them go.

"Shall we go back?" Charles asked Diana.

"Of course," she said.

They went out again, waved, and Charles led her back inside. The crowd had not had enough. Three times more they returned, brought back by the continued and insistent cheers. Diana whispered to him that she felt like an actor in a big opening night hit.

Cries of "Kiss! Kiss! Kiss!" echoed in the courtyard. Diana and Charles smiled down, laughing and waving, and then Diana held hands with Charles, waved again, and finally turned to Charles helplessly.

"They are trying to get us to kiss," Charles said.

"I tried to ask you."

"Well, how about it?"

"Why ever not?"

And they did.

It was the first public kiss on the palace balcony, the first time any member of a royal family had ever bussed on demand for a crowd of their subjects. But it was a loving kiss, a tender kiss, and one that brought even more cheers and whistles from the crowd of lookers. Someone in the crowd broke out a huge banner and waved it above the sea of heads:

LOVE IS CHARLIE AND DI

Diana drew Charles back into the palace for the wedding

breakfast which had, as its centerpiece, a five-tiered wedding cake. Weighing two hundred twenty-four pounds, it had marzipan and ivory-white icing on the top. It was four-and-a-half feet high.

Meanwhile, two of the wedding guests were out in the courtyard taking part in a typical royal family prank. They were Charles's brothers Andrew and Edward. From the staff they got hold of a dozen blue-and-silver balloons emblazoned with the Prince of Wales's emblem; they begged, borrowed, or stole a lipstick from one of the ladies-in-waiting; and began to rig the royal carriage in which Charles and Diana were to ride to Waterloo Station after the breakfast.

With the lipstick, Andrew scrawled JUST MARRIED across a placard on the back of the buggy, and Edward drew two hearts and arrows. When Charles and Diana hurried out into the courtyard to leave, the wedding guests threw rose petals down on them as they made their way to the landau that would take them to Waterloo Station. Diana saw the sign on the back of the carriage and laughed.

She had changed into a soft, cantaloupe-color traveling outfit, a five-strand pearl choker at her throat, and a perky straw hat with ostrich feathers to top it off. Charles was in a gray-pinstripe business suit and tie.

Two footmen, dressed in black top hats, scarlet jackets, black trousers, and white gloves, sat behind them gazing out over the crowd. The riders were dressed in military helmets, black velvet jackets, white trousers, riding boots, and gloves.

At a signal, the open landau started up, with the riders guiding it out of the courtyard and through the gate into the waiting crowd. As the black landau with its red wheels rattled into sight in full view of the crowd, another loud cheer went up, mixed with laughter.

"They look like two nine-to-fivers heading for a week at

Brighton," one spectator boomed out.

Diana sat beside Charles breathing in the adulation and the excitement. He took her hand and held it on his knee. She squeezed his hand and returned the intimate pressure. They began to wind slowly and leisurely through The Mall and down to Waterloo Station across the Thames.

Television cameras followed them every step of the way. At Waterloo Station, Diana saw their own private train standing there waiting for them on Platform 12, the famous "tryst" train, ready to take them out to Hampshire.

They alighted from the landau and stood hand in hand at the station, waving to the crowds. Lord Maclean, the Lord Chamberlain, who had guided the wedding arrangements from the beginning, was standing there waiting to help them into the train. When he smiled at Diana, she reached over impulsively and planted an enthusiastic kiss on his cheek.

Quickly the two of them climbed into the train. In moments, even before they were comfortably seated, it was on its way. They sat in the middle coach of the three-carriage train with electric locomotive. The train moved quickly north to Broadlands.

At Romsey, Diana and Charles had to disembark for the ride to the Mountbatten estate which was to be the site of their honeymoon. There they were forced to run a gauntlet of more enthusiastic crowds—predominantly children this time—wanting to greet them and watch them drive off to Broadlands.

Journalists and photographers were standing around the locked gates of the estate, trying to winnow out scraps of information. The river Test flowed along the edge of the estate; it was expected that Charles would be fishing there perhaps on the following morning. Would he appear for the press?

He would not promise one way or the other.

Finally, as the huge iron gates of the 6,000-acre parkland of Broadlands clanged shut behind them, Diana turned to Charles and said what every bride has always said to her husband at the beginning of the honeymoon:

"Honey! Alone at last!"

They laughed and kissed long and lingeringly.

19

She awoke feeling fresh and bright, and stretched luxuriantly. Although she felt tired, she was somehow completely refreshed and rejuvenated. It was enough to be alive and joyously happy. For a moment she could not remember where she was.

Then, in a flood, the joyous truth flowed over her. She reached out her hand to reassure herself that she was not simply dreaming once again, and found his solid presence close beside her. She turned and thought mischievously of awakening him, but decided to let him sleep.

She reached for her ring finger and felt the gold wedding band that he had slipped on it the day before during that endless and magnificent ceremony. She watched him sleeping quietly—he was so different from the night before, so completely relaxed now and peaceful; and she knew that any fears she might have had as to his love for her were now completely put to rest. He had proved it to her in the most direct way possible.

"Diana, love—are you happy?"

She was startled. "I didn't know you were awake."

"Not really awake. Just dozing." He turned and drew her closer to him. "I don't know where I ever got the impression that you were a simple little teenager. You certainly proved me wrong last night."

She blushed and slapped at his shoulder. "I didn't think you'd mind."

"I don't!" He laughed. "You never believe in half measures, do you?"

She lay back and smiled at the ceiling. "I've been in love with you all my life, Charles. And I want only to please you."

He lifted himself on his elbow and looked down into her face. "You do. Completely."

She felt his lips on hers.

After rising in a leisurely fashion several hours later, Diana led Charles out of the house and they walked hand in hand along the numerous paths of the estate. They passed the old William and Mary stable building, with the Japanese gun in front of it, and then wandered down to the river Test to watch it flow along.

"They've dammed it up, you know," Charles said.

"Why?"

"You can float things down through the estate that might prove dangerous. Things that go 'boom.'"

Diana looked into Charles's serious blue eyes and shuddered. His arm tightened around her waist. She closed her eyes.

One of the security agents appeared suddenly in the woods near them, but as soon as he realized he had been seen he vanished. Charles cast a longing look at the river Test and then reluctantly drew himself away from it.

"Go on, go on!" laughed Diana.

Charles looked innocent. "Go on and what?"

"Get your fishing gear out! I know you're dying to try out the trout run."

Charles quirked an eyebrow. "Well, it *is* called the river Test."

"Charles!" She slapped him affectionately and they both burst into laughter.

Back at the house they picked up the fishing gear that had been carefully laid out for Charles by his valet. While Diana watched, he began casting in the water, but had little luck. In fact, an hour later he declared himself hors de combat. Damming up the river had prevented bombs from entering, he said, but it had also prevented trout from entering.

Later on they found an old rowboat in the boathouse. Charles spent the next hour and a half rowing his bride up and down the Test.

That night they ate dinner under an enormous and splendid chandelier in the dining room hung with a rich panoply of four Van Dyck originals and a painting of Emma Hamilton, looking slightly bleary-eyed, possibly from champagne, gazing down at them from another wall.

Diana was fascinated by the eighteenth-century architecture of the house, with its quaint Ionic pillars and its very elaborate furnishings. There was a Wedgwood Room, done in robin's-egg blue, with the walls decorated in delicate white designs, and the tables and chairs all in the traditional Wedgwood blue and white. There was The Salon, decorated in delicate gilt, classic style, with fragile divans and chairs arranged before a fireplace topped by a huge ornamental mirror that made the room look twice the size it was.

Charles was far more fascinated by the stables, with their green doors and round second-story windows. He kept watching the horses feeding and looking out at him.

Eventually Diana managed to get him back to the house,

where they spent their afternoon in the sun by the large swimming pool.

"I was a champion diver, I'll have you know, back in school," Diana told Charles. She tried the diving board, soaring up into the air and down into the water without making a ripple.

"Beautiful, love!" Charles cried. He followed her in, not quite so gracefully.

Soon they were splashing about at one another. Charles tried ducking her only once, finding that she could slip out of his hands like an eel, and then come back and hold him down with her own strong hands. After their swim, they relaxed by the pool, drinking champagne.

Nothing intruded upon their privacy. It was really the first peace and quiet they had experienced together since the day they had begun to fall in love at Balmoral Castle on the river Dee.

Too soon the first phase of their honeymoon was over, and the time came for them to leave Broadlands. On Saturday morning, three days after the wedding, they rose early and drove over with their detective escort and baggage to Eastleigh Airport near Southampton. Charles took over control of the turboprop Andover, one of the three airplanes in the Queen's Flight, taking off without delay for the seven-hour trip to Gibraltar. He even personally piloted the plane for part of the flight.

At Gibraltar Airport it was obvious that they were going to be in for crowds and shouting again. People were shoving against the hurricane fence and threatening to flatten it as the newlyweds ducked out of the Andover and got into an open brown Triumph that was to take them to the yacht *Britannia*.

Cheers went up as they drove through the gate and into the streets of the town. The sidewalks were jammed. The air resounded with shouts; it was brilliant with waving Union Jacks, pennants, flags, and the sky was thick with confetti. Balloons were going up everywhere. The red telephone booths of Gibraltar Town, the blue-uniformed bobbies, the trim little pubs, and the red, white, and blue banners seemed more like England to Diana than some parts of Britain itself.

She had dressed in a loose-fitting white dress with a floral pattern. Charles was in a plain business suit. The band played "Rule Britannia" as they drove slowly along through the crowded thoroughfares, waving at the hysterical crowds.

Diana could hardly believe the sight that greeted her in Algeciras Bay. It was the *Britannia*, the royal yacht she had seen and been on several times before—a complete seagoing resort complete with swimming pool, ballroom, chapel, theater, and a dining room that seated forty. In appearance the craft was brilliant with color and glitter, her hull a swath of royal blue, red, and gold, with a royal coat of arms on the bow and the royal cipher on the stern.

When they alighted from their open Triumph, the day was already beginning to dwindle into twilight. The bay was aglitter with the blaze of the lowering sun and the brilliant colors of the *Britannia*. Spanish fishing boats from the area dotted the bay, simply watching the spectacle of the royal departure.

As Their Royal Highnesses mounted the gangplank, they were not piped aboard the yacht; only the Queen deserved that honor. Immediately the order was given to set sail. The 12,000-horsepower, twin-shaft turbine engines began turning over to push the yacht out of the harbor past the famous North Mole.

Diana and Charles were standing hand in hand on the afterdeck as the sun sank into the west and the strains of "Rule Britannia" faded into the distance on the shore. Soon land was almost out of sight and the yacht began to move lazily along in its own graceful, ponderous way, pitching only slightly to the Mediterranean's easy roll.

They went down to see their living quarters. Diana was ecstatic. The main drawing room was decorated with typical English country charm—off-white walls, needlepoint rugs, and chairs covered with floral chintz. Charles loved the golden urn commemorating Nelson's victory at Trafalgar, and admired the set of shark's teeth from the Solomon Islands.

In the royal bedroom they found that their orders had been carefully carried out. During Princess Anne's honeymoon with Captain Mark Phillips, the two of them had been forced to lash together two twin beds in the royal suite to serve as a marriage couch. Diana and Charles had ordered a substitution of furniture for the royal bedroom. The twin lashup had been removed and in its place now stood a single queen-sized bed.

And the honeymoon—interrupted for only an eighteen-hour period—continued aboard ship.

Even though there were 276 officers and men present, Diana and Charles found plenty of time alone with one another. With the complete run of the yacht, they took advantage of the various forms of entertainment on the ship, using the swimming pool as much as they wanted.

Charles seemed to be turning over a new leaf. Usually up at six o'clock and jogging around the deck, he learned to stay in bed late and enjoy himself. He even napped in the afternoon, an unheard-of departure from the spartan regimen he always followed.

Diana was still attired in her bikini one afternoon when she decided to explore the ship. She walked into the officer's mess at the moment members of the crew were returning from the showers. Most of them were naked except for towels wrapped around their hips.

"I'm afraid you shouldn't be here, Ma'am," said one of the crewmen politely, his face beet red.

Diana didn't turn a hair. "It's all right. I'm a married woman now, aren't I?"

Indeed she was.

Diana relaxed and blossomed in Charles's obvious love for her. It was during those quiet, summery days that the two of them really got to know one another. The courtship itself, both admitted, had been hectic and strained. Now they were able to indulge in an intimate, comfortable, leisurely type of romancing that had been denied them before.

As they grew closer to one another, bound now by physical intimacy as well as psychological, the *Britannia* steamed its way around the Med, passing along the coast of Algeria, Tunisia, southern Italy, and then up into the Greek Islands.

During its first days, the yacht made no stops. Diana and Charles chatted unhurriedly about music, about art, about literature. They found that they shared the same love of light music, soft lights, and beautiful flowers. Of course they had always known *something* about each other's dislikes and enthusiasms, but the intimate knowledge took time to assimilate.

"I'm not a very educated person," Diana confessed once to Charles. "I don't have to tell you that. You've got to teach me things."

Charles chuckled. "I've had a good education—probably the best there is. If I do say so myself, I'm the first Prince of Wales ever to graduate from University. And I've read lots of books. I love to read." He reached over and lifted her chin until her eyes were looking directly into his. "I want to tell you that there is nothing you can learn in any book ever written, or in any lecture ever delivered, that will make you any more dear or beloved to me than you are right now."

She began to cry. But the tears were happy ones. Her lack of education did frighten her, nevertheless. "Don't let me be stupid, Charles!"

"You couldn't be stupid if you tried. You've got a confidence and a self-reliance that even I wish I had. Besides, you're probably the most beautiful woman—I mean, really, radiantly, glowingly beautiful—in the world. At least, that I've ever seen."

She eyed him wryly. "If you're trying to get me all excited for a little playing around, Charles, you're succeeding!"

"That's another pleasant surprise. Darling, I went into this thing with my eyes wide open. I mean, it was like being *arranged* into marriage. Oh, you were approved by everybody. That was fine. But I never thought you'd turn out the way you have!"

She drew him against her and kissed him spontaneously.

"I didn't really know what it would be to—to fall in love!" Charles drew back and blinked, realizing what he had said. "That's the truth, love. I used to joke about love. 'If that's what love is,' I said. Just to be smart. In front of everybody, too." Charles shook his head. "Damn it, you've made a believer of an agnostic."

"I've always loved you, Charles," she said.

"At the risk of being too sentimental, Diana—I now know what love really is. It's you, love—and what you bring to me."

They ate most of their meals informally on the veranda deck or in the sun lounge. Silent crewmen in monkey jackets delivered the food and vanished. Several of the evening meals they took together at one end of a fifty-six seat table in the royal dining room. They ate with their laps protected by napkins artistically folded into the lines of the Union Jack. Outside, in the anteroom, a string quartet played romantic melodies to eat by. After the meal Diana and Charles leaned on the railing to look out into the phosphorescence of the Mediterranean Ocean.

On the sixth day of the cruise, their first landfall occurred. It was August 7. They anchored a mile off the coast of Ithaca in the Greek Islands at eight o'clock in the evening. Diana and Charles put ashore into a secluded cove for a swim. A boat in the Greek Navy stood on patrol nearby until they had finished.

"This is the home of Odysseus," Charles told Diana.

"Is it?"

By August 10 they were near the island of Thera in the Aegean Sea, off southern Greece in the Cyclades Islands. Two days later they were anchored off Port Said, Egypt, at the tip of the Sinai Peninsula, at the head of the Suez Canal.

On the evening of August 12, President Anwar el-Sadat of Egypt and his wife Jihan arrived to spend the evening and dine with Charles and Diana. It was Diana's first opportunity to play royal hostess. Sadat was enchanted with her. Jihan, his wife, had been born in Yorkshire, and knew England intimately. When the guests left the yacht, Diana impulsively leaned over and kissed Jihan on the cheek. It was a most unusual way for any member of the royal family to salute the wife of the head of a foreign state, even if she was a fellow Briton. But the kiss was taken in the spirit in which it was given—pleasantly, spontaneously, and affectionately.

The *Britannia* entered the Suez Canal and steamed down into the Red Sea where Diana and Charles snorkeled together in the coral reefs. On the last night of the two-week cruise, the crew gave a "concert"—at which Diana played the piano to accompany a sing-along that tended to be a trifle rowdy but at which she laughed as much as did Charles.

On August 14, the royal couple landed at Port Said and were driven to an Egyptian military airport close by. There they boarded a British plane, and flew home to Britain.

The honeymoon was indeed over, but the marriage was beginning to take on a very satisfactory and permanent shape. Both Prince and Princess had changed the other during the honeymoon's intimate hours.

Diana was a little more sure of herself, a little more self-possessed, a little more thinned-down and sophisticated in appearance.

Charles was a great deal more relaxed, much less intense and withdrawn, and he was obviously in love.

Within weeks, the first tragedy connected with the honeymoon occurred. Egyptian President Anwar el-Sadat was assassinated in Egypt. When Diana heard the news, she collapsed in tears. "How can people behave like that?" she cried.

Charles refused to let her accompany him to the funeral, although she wanted to go. She drove down to Heathrow with him and wept as she kissed him goodbye. Her original antipathy to the two full-time bodyguards who were always around her began to abate at that moment.

Then someone slashed her portrait in the National Portrait Gallery. The IRA? Some antimonarchy freak? A crazy?

Another anonymous person mailed a letter bomb to Prince Charles. Luckily it was intercepted at Buckingham Palace before he opened it.

When Diana was made Princess of Wales, a group of demonstrators hit the maroon Rolls-Royce limousine in which she traveled with a paint bomb.

But that was the extent of the bad news. The good news came on November 6. "THE PRINCESS OF WALES IS EXPECTING A BABY IN JUNE," said the announcement from Buckingham Palace.

Although she had swallowed her intense antipathy for blood sports as a concession to her husband's love of them, Diana had never changed her mind about shooting animals. For the sake of marital harmony, she continued to accompany him on pheasant shoots at Sandringham. But one day, on a bitter cold morning, with the wind blowing and an overcast sky threatening above, Diana suddenly had had enough.

As the rest of the group moved ahead, Diana hung back. Charles left his mother and father and brothers and went over to ask her what was the matter.

Diana drew him aside and whispered in his ear. He made a face and wheeled away to rejoin the royal party. Diana watched him go and lost her temper.

"You know I didn't want to come here in the first place," she shouted at him. "What am I doing here?"

The Queen heard. She turned around in shock. Charles stopped in his tracks, spun around, and yelled back at her: "Stop complaining and get on with it!"

Diana flared up. Charles immediately ordered the royal staff out of earshot and stalked back to confront her. The royal couple continued to argue in fierce low tones that could not be heard by anyone else.

By afternoon, they were back in each other's good graces. The anger of the moment had passed over.

"I'm sorry, Charles. I simply wasn't feeling myself."

"That's all right, love. It was a bad day."

But two days later her feelings once again surfaced. On the morning of that shoot, she set her foot down.

"I'm not going with you!" she told him.

"Come, now. Don't be so childish!" Charles snapped back.

"I'm *not* childish!" Diana cried. "I hate killing animals!"

"It's part of our life. You've got to accept it. You don't have to shoot. But I think you should be with us."

Diana held back the tears and went up to her room to dress. She would not do anything to harm her marriage. She swallowed her pride, put on a good face, and joined the royal family once again. She thought of it now as part of her duty.

Gradually Diana began to withdraw from public ceremonies after her pregnancy was announced. She visited here and there, making mostly token appearances, but spent much of her time within the circle of the royal family, who treated her as a genuine treasure.

She had established a particularly good rapport with Prince Philip, whose face actually beamed whenever she spoke to him. And with the Queen she frequently went for long walks, discussing not only the intimacies of pregnancy, but her personal relationship with Charles.

She also found that Princess Margaret and Charles were much closer than she had suspected before she had married into the family. The two of them—Princess Margaret and Princess Diana—frequently had long and intimate chats about everything from royal life in general to specific people in the family.

Highgrove had proved a disappointment to Diana. Almost from the beginning, she felt a bit cramped in the house, large as it was. Immediately she began worrying about what would happen once the royal heir or heiress was born. Almost immediately she began searching for a larger place to live—and found it at Belton Hall, almost seventy miles away. Belton Hall has twenty-six bedrooms, as against Highgrove's nine.

As for her pregnancy, Diana reacted pretty much the way any young woman of the 1980s was reacting. She continued to dress informally in the heart of the family, oftentimes wearing jeans and sweaters just as she had done at school and in London. And she made headlines one day by taking a shopping trip into Tetbury and buying, among other things, winegum—a bubblegum that had always been a favorite of hers.

As her days of confinement approached, Diana and Charles discussed the coming event not in terms of the specific birth but in terms of the future.

"We'll want more than just one, of course," Diana said.

Charles was in agreement on that.

"I think we should have three within the first five years," Diana went on. And so it was finally stated in an interview in the newspapers.

Diana learned another interesting fact during one of her routine visits to the doctor. A medical scan was performed on her to monitor the growth and condition of her baby. The scan involved photographs of the fetus. Its sex was determined as that of male, according to the physicians in charge of the scan.

That story made the pages of *The Observer*, a newspaper more respected than the tabloids and sensation rags. But when the facts were checked with Buckingham Palace, there was no confirmation at all.

Even Diana was not one to put too much faith on the medical scan. How did they know, anyway? "We'll simply have to wait until June to find out if it's a boy or a girl," she said cheerfully.

And on June 21, 1982, of course, the truth was out.

A new King was born.